The Last Ride

Of

Bonnie and Clyde

Copyright © 2013 by David J. Pietras

All rights reserved. No part of this publication may be reproduced, distributed, or transmitted in any form or by any means, including photocopying, recording, or other electronic or mechanical methods, without the prior written permission of the publisher, except in the case of brief quotations embodied in critical reviews and certain other noncommercial uses permitted by copyright law. For permission requests, write to the publisher, addressed "Attention: Permissions Coordinator," at the web site below.

http://mrdavepp.wix.com/davidpietras

Cover design by David Pietras

1 2 3 4 5 6 7 8 9 10 13

ISBN-13: 978-1494789794
ISBN-10: 1494789795

Prologue

Bonnie and Clyde were meant for each other. And they clung to each other while they fought back against the elements. These elements were destitution and a government they took for its face value. They were children of a nationwide economic depression that not unlike France in the late 1700s had its upheavals and those who tried to keep small the size and impact of the upheavals.

Anger dwelt within Clyde, having been born ragged and made more ragged by the Depression. He sometimes killed in cold blood, and always tried to justify the murders as if he had a right to pull that trigger, thus releasing somehow the seething that built up like a volcano deep inside him. Perhaps he actually believed in his own special privilege. As the fame of Bonnie and Clyde grew, they shot their way out of police loops, each time growing tighter and tighter, and claimed that the "laws" they killed just happened to get in the way between their fiery outcry and the rest of the country. Their killings were not personal, they contended. But, the government took them personal. And Bonnie and her man were marked for death.

Depression had lowered a hideous shroud over the nation. The American Dream collapsed along with Wall Street in 1929. Pride of freedom became a joke. "The country's money simply declined by 38 percent," explains E.R. Milner, author of The Lives and Times of Bonnie and Clyde. "Gaunt dazed men roamed the city streets seeking jobs...Breadlines and soup kitchens became jammed. (In rural areas) foreclosures forced more than 38 percent of farmers from their lands (while simultaneously) a catastrophic drought struck the Great Plains...By the time Bonnie and Clyde became well known, many had felt the capitalistic system had been abused by big business and government officials...Now here were Bonnie and Clyde striking back."

While they terrorized banks and store owners in five states Texas, Oklahoma, Missouri, Louisiana, and New Mexico Americans thrilled to their "Robin Hood" adventures. The presence of a female, Bonnie, escalated the sincerity of their intentions to make them something unique and individual even at times heroic and above similar activities of all-male motor bandits like John Dillinger, "Baby Face" Nelson and "Pretty Boy" Floyd.

Historian Jonathan Davis, in an excellent A&E Cable Network-produced Biography on the two bandits, says of Bonnie and Clyde's crimes, "Anybody who robbed banks or fought the law were really living out some secret fantasies on a large part of the public."

Even more than their insurgence against their status in life was Bonnie and Clyde's devotion to their own. With police and government detectives constantly on their trails, sometimes literally by inches, they time and time again risked their own lives to protect the other. Says Marie Barrow, Clyde's sister, in Biography, "They never worried about anything else but each other."

When on the lam, they found time to visit their Dallas-area families, risking capture more than once. Marie asserts that her brother and father had concocted their own signal to let the families know when the outlaws were in town: Clyde would drive the latest of his stolen automobiles in front of the Barrow service station and from the car toss a soda pop bottle containing directions to a place of rendezvous. "My mother would fix them something to eat," she adds.

Clyde Barrow and Bonnie Parker

In their getaway cars, Clyde and Bonnie habitually carried a Kodak box camera; they loved to pose in dramatic tableaux wielding shotguns and revolvers, self-parodying the gangster image they realized they had earned. More than that, they loved to pose together, embraced or kissing, having other gang members do the snapping. When they died, the police found an undeveloped roll of film under their car seat photos of them together, looking adventurous and deeply in love.

They knew they were going to die, maybe next week, maybe next month, maybe in the morning. They never pretended they might be the only exception to the standard, "Crime doesn't pay". But, because they knew their time was limited their crime spree lasted less than two years they decided to let all hell break loose in the meantime to whoop and holler it up till death do them part. Bonnie's last request to her mother was, "Don't bring me to a funeral parlor. Bring me home."

The last two years of their lives, once they met, were a whirly-gig. Never-ending highways burning in the Southwest sun; dusty back roads; the scorch of over-heated radiators; the burn of rubber; the stifled campiness of one car after another; their only air the hot breeze they channeled through rolled-down car windows. A fast life, a die-young life. And they wouldn't have traded it for the world.

They were Bonnie and Clyde.

Biography

Over a two-year period from 1932-34, during the height of the Great Depression in America, Bonnie & Clyde evolved from petty thieves to nationally known bank robbers and murderers.

Their robbery of banks and store owners, in a rural America ravaged by farm foreclosures and bankruptcies, led to their exploits and relationship being romanticized by a burgeoning 'yellow' press. In reality, at the time of their death, their gang was believed to be responsible for at least 13 murders, including two policemen, several robberies and burglaries and assorted kidnappings, abductions and woundings.

Bonnie Elizabeth Parker and Clyde Chestnut Barrow traveled the Central United States with their gang during the Great Depression. At times the gang included Buck Barrow, Blanche Barrow, Raymond Hamilton, W.D. Jones, Joe Palmer, Ralph Fults, and Henry Methvin. Their exploits captured the attention of the American public during the "public enemy era" between 1931 and 1934. Though known today for his dozen-or-so bank robberies, Barrow in fact preferred to rob small stores or rural gas stations. The gang is believed to have killed at least nine police officers and committed several civilian murders. The couple themselves were eventually ambushed and killed in North Louisiana by law officers. Their reputation was cemented in American pop folklore by Arthur Penn's 1967 film *Bonnie and Clyde*. Even during their lifetimes, the couple's depiction in the press was at considerable odds with the hardscrabble reality of their life on the road—particularly in the case of Parker. Though she was present at a hundred or more felonies during her two years as Barrow's companion, she was not the machine gun-wielding cartoon killer portrayed in the newspapers, newsreels, and pulp detective magazines of the day. Gang member W. D. Jones was unsure whether he had ever seen her fire at officers. Parker's reputation as a cigar-smoking gun moll grew out of a playful snapshot found by police at an abandoned hideout, released to the press, and published nationwide; while she did chain-smoke Camel cigarettes, she was not a cigar smoker.

Author-historian, Jeff Guinn, explains that it was the release of these very photos that put the outlaws on the media map and launched their legend: "John Dillinger had matinee-idol good looks and Pretty Boy Floyd had the best possible nickname, but the Joplin photos introduced new criminal superstars with the most titillating trademark of all—illicit sex. Clyde Barrow and Bonnie Parker were wild and young, and undoubtedly slept together. Without Bonnie, the media outside Texas might have dismissed Clyde as a gun-toting punk, if it ever considered him at all. With her sassy photographs, Bonnie supplied the sex-appeal, the oomph, that allowed the two of them to transcend the small-scale thefts and needless killings that actually comprised their criminal careers."

Bonnie Parker

Bonnie Elizabeth Parker (October 1, 1910 – May 23, 1934) was born in Rowena, Texas, the second of three children. Her father, Charles Parker, a bricklayer, died when Bonnie was four. Her mother, Emma Krause, moved with the children to her parents' home in Cement City, an industrial suburb of Dallas, where she found work as a seamstress. Her maternal grandfather, Frank Krause, came from Germany. Parker was one of the best students in her high school, winning top prizes in spelling, writing, and public speaking. As an adult, her fondness for writing found expression in poems such as "The Story of Suicide Sal" and "The Trail's End" (known since as "The Story of Bonnie and Clyde").

In her second year of high school, Parker met Roy Thornton. They dropped out of school and were married on September 25, 1926, six days before Parker's 16th birthday. Their marriage, marked by his frequent absences and brushes with the law, was short-lived. After January 1929, their paths never crossed again. However, they were never divorced, and Parker was wearing Thornton's wedding ring when she died. Thornton was in prison in 1934 when he learned of her death. His reaction was, "I'm glad they went out like they did. It's much better than being caught."

Bonnie & Roy Thornton

In 1929, after the breakdown of her marriage and before her first meeting with Clyde Barrow in January 1930, Parker lived with her mother and worked as a waitress in Dallas. One of her regular customers in the café was postal worker Ted Hinton, who would join the Dallas Sheriff's Department in 1932 and, as a posse member, would participate in her ambush in 1934. In the diary she kept briefly early in 1929, she wrote of her loneliness, her impatience with life in provincial Dallas, and her love of talking pictures.

Clyde Barrow

Clyde Chestnut Barrow (March 24, 1909 – May 23, 1934) was born in Ellis County, Texas, near Telico, a town just south of Dallas. He was the fifth of seven children of Henry Basil Barrow (1874–1957) and Cumie T. Walker (1874–1943), a poor farming family that emigrated, piecemeal, to Dallas in the early 1920s as part of a wave of resettlement from the impoverished nearby farms to the urban slum known as West Dallas. The Barrows spent their first months in West Dallas living under their wagon. When father Henry had earned enough money to buy a tent, it was a major step up for the family.

Clyde stood 5'7," weighed 130 pounds, slicked back his thick brown hair in the style of the day, and parted it on the left. His eye color matched his hair. Women found him attractive. He came into this world as one of many children born to dirt-poor tenant farmer parents barely making a living on the cotton fields of Teleco, Texas. Moving with his parents, brothers and sisters to the Dallas outskirts, where his father ran a gas station (in which the family members crowded as one into a tiny back room), Clyde quickly learned to abhor poverty. Bored and poor, he too knew life had something more to offer.

Clyde was first arrested in late 1926, after running when police confronted him over a rental car he had failed to return on time. His second arrest, with brother Marvin "Buck" Barrow, came soon after, this time for possession of stolen goods (turkeys). Despite having legitimate jobs during the period 1927 through 1929, he also cracked safes, robbed stores, and stole cars. After sequential arrests in 1928 and 1929, he was sent to Eastham Prison Farm in April 1930. While in prison, Barrow beat to death another inmate who had repeatedly assaulted him sexually. It was Clyde Barrow's first killing.

It was here; behind the furthest column that Clyde had killed his first man,
a vicious building tender named Ed "Big Ed" Crowder. The 6' tall 200 pound Ed
had been preying upon the young Clyde Barrow who decided that he wasn't going to take it anymore.

Paroled in February 1932, Barrow emerged from Eastham a hardened and bitter criminal. His sister Marie said "Something awful sure must have happened to him in prison, because he wasn't the same person when he got out." A fellow inmate, Ralph Fults, said he watched him "change from a schoolboy to a rattlesnake."

In his post-Eastham career, he focused on smaller jobs, robbing grocery stores and gas stations, at a rate far outpacing the mere ten to fifteen bank robberies attributed to him and the Barrow Gang. Barrow's favored weapon was the M1918 Browning Automatic Rifle (called a BAR). According to John Neal Phillips, Barrow's goal in life was not to gain fame or fortune from robbing banks, but to seek revenge against the Texas prison system for the abuses he suffered while serving time.

First meeting

There are several versions of the story describing Bonnie and Clyde's first meeting, but the most credible version indicates that Bonnie Parker met Clyde Barrow in January 1930 at a friend's house. Parker was out of work and was staying in West Dallas to assist a female friend with a broken arm. Barrow dropped by the girl's house while Parker was supposedly in the kitchen making hot chocolate.

When they met, both were smitten immediately; most historians believe Parker joined Barrow because she was in love. She remained a loyal companion to him as they carried out their crime spree and awaited the violent deaths they viewed as inevitable.

Clyde never forgot his first days in West Dallas. Thinking of them in adulthood made him bitter. Only a child then, he recalled the humiliating experience of his family being forced to live for days under a viaduct with other transient families who had no place to go and no money to get them there even if they had. When it rained, the Barrows jumbled together with maybe forty others watching the ground below the overpass turn from clay into mud, and into a little river where they otherwise would have been able to sleep that night. Henry and Cummie Barrow had left the cotton fields back at Teleco and had come to Dallas with their eight children (of which Clyde was the fifth) to seek employment. Within a couple of weeks, due to insistence, Papa Barrow found work at the Star gas station on Eagle Ford Road. Not much money, maybe, but it provided the family with a roof and four walls the one-room storage area behind the front counter littered with Dr. Pepper and Nehi signs.

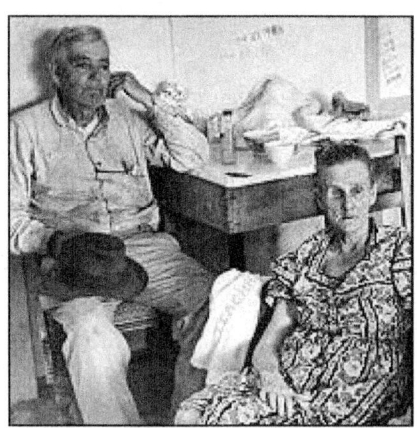
Clyde Barrow's parents

Cummie thanked the Lord her Henry had escaped the grueling heat and torturous labor that had been slowly killing him as a cotton picker. Maybe they ate meatless stew for weeks on end now, and sometimes went to bed hungry, but at least her kids were able to attend school, Cedar Valley, and would get an education so they wouldn't have to endure any more downpours.

Clyde and his brother Ivan, whom everyone called "Buck," generally skipped classes, though. They would wander for hours in the back streets of Dallas and engage in fisticuffs with the other truants who, like Clyde, saw no future at Cedar Valley.

While the wayward Barrow boys were ditching school, across the tracks in Cement City, a cute little redhead with ringlets and a too-mature swivel in her hips for a teenager was attracting the attention of the local boys in Cement City High School. Bonnie Parker was a capable student, her teachers noted, and they saw her with her mother and grandmother every Sunday at the First Baptist Church in town. The only trouble is she seemed a little too preoccupied with Roy Thornton, one of the "bad boys."

Much to her mother's woes, Thornton was an after-school staple walking her home daily to Olive Street. No one, not even Mrs. Parker, was really surprised when Bonnie quit school and eloped at age 16.

Clyde Barrow and older brother Buck dropped out, too, to spend their days sleeping and their nights yahooing with the hillbillies who hung out in the pool halls, at freight yards and on the corners of West Dallas. Bored, they made their own excitement and, much to the chagrin of the local police, excitement meant something illegal. At first, this translated as small stuff, breaking a window here, stealing a bag of candy there. But, boredom escalated and so did their "excitement".

One night, the "Terrible Barrows" (as the neighbors took to calling the duo) stole a flivver and cruised the dark boulevards of nearby Denton. They wanted money and, with a little moonshine under their belt, decided to burgle one of the many shops fronting Main Street. They chose the Motor Mark Garage. Pulling their car, headlights off, through an alley, they parked behind the place and jimmied the shop's lock until it snapped. Greeting them in the alcove was a small safe, bathed in moonlight that poured in through the window. It looked inviting. More so, it looked portable. Hoisting it, they carried it out and tossed it onto the back seat of their auto, laughing at the incredible ease of this job.

A scouting patrol car, however, had earlier spotted the suspicious vehicle and, before Clyde and Buck could travel two blocks with the ungainly prize, they found themselves being pursued. Panicky, driver Buck crashed the car into a lamp-post; the two brothers lit out. Clyde escaped through a succession of Denton backyards, but Buck had stumbled. The police nabbed him. Refusing to name his accomplice, they took him to Denton's courthouse and booked him for robbery. In an ensuing trial, he received several years in Huntsville State Prison.

Clyde might have learned from this fiasco and his brother's literal stumbling into constabulary hands. He didn't. The night after the foiled theft, he and his friends were out burgling other stores in neighboring Waco.

Just as unlucky as the oldest Barrow boy had been with the law was Roy Thornton, Bonnie Parker's young husband. About the same time Buck was being incarcerated, he too was slapped with a multiple-year jail term for thievery. Bonnie moved back into her grandmother's house and took a job as a waitress at Marco's Cafe in the heart of Dallas. She was more angry at Roy than she missed him; she had warned him time and again, "Be careful!". Now here she was, reduced to catering to hungry, louting truckers with heart tattoos who slapped her behind and passed crude comments as she wiggled by with heavy soup trays. One of her nicer customers was a town policeman named Ted Hinton; he never flirted and seemed to mind his own business, merely acknowledging her with a friendly hello at breakfast every morning.

Bonnie Parker

"(Bonnie) was a very pretty young woman with taffy-colored hair that glistened red in the sun and with a complexion that was fair and tended to freckle," he wrote years later. In his book, *Ambush*, co-authored with Larry Grove, he admitted he had had an attraction to her. "Photographs...failed to do justice to her looks. The clothes she wore viewed by later generations tend to diminish the sparkle she had when I knew her...Bonnie could turn heads."

Though Hinton and Bonnie rarely spoke those mornings in the cafe, and it is doubtful they knew each other's last names, both would, in less than five years, come together on a country highway in northern Louisiana. Bonnie would be dead. Hinton would be one of a group of lawmen who shot her.

But, in the late Fall of 1929, there was no harbinger of death, lest it be in the auspicious form of the gremlin who kicked the air out of the nation's money gullet. Both Bonnie Parker and Clyde Barrow saw, from their respective angles, the quivering beginnings of what would be called in time the Great Depression. They saw the "Out of Business" signs being nailed to the doors of once prosperous Dallas shops, saw the clutters of furniture piled in front of homes whose families lost their daily bread and the rent money; saw the gray procession of truck farmers on the roads around Dallas thumbing their way to Anywhere, USA, where, because they were tossed off their land here, began a search for new beginnings elsewhere.

Clyde fumed at the sight. He knew what it was to go hungry and cussed President Hoover and the rest of the damn cigar-chomping politicians who were allowing dungaree America go to the dogs. The government was taking away the lives of all these people well, he would take back something from the government for a change. And he'd do it as he always had done it: by slapping the face of Uncle Sam.

Throughout neighboring McClennan and mostly Waco counties, he and an assembled band of ruffians terrorized small shop owners through burglaries and face-to-face holdups, and, as if daring the law to react, boasted his crimes to anyone who listened. Just before Christmas of 1929, authorities determined to fully investigate the activities on one Clyde Chestnut Barrow with intent to apprehend once enough evidence was gathered.

Not realizing that he was in danger, Clyde drifted around Dallas as slowly as the days crawled for the poor at Yuletide. One evening, hearing that a sister of one his huckleberries had slipped and fallen on an ice patch and broken an arm; he decided to pay her a visit to cheer her up. After salutations were complete, he asked her what the clatter was in the kitchen.

"That's my girlfriend," she said, "mixing up some hot chocolate. Go in and say hello. Her name's Bonnie Parker."

It was love at first sight, for both of them, insanity born over Ovaltine. Almost forgetting about their unfortunate mutual friend, Bonnie and Clyde talked well into the late hours. And they continued to see each other, almost daily over the next couple of months.

The Jailbreak in Waco

It is believed that Bonnie, now suddenly in love, refreshed with life and having forgotten about her loser husband, even drove the gang's car while Clyde and his friends pilfered cash registers and shoplifted.

On February 12, 1930, Clyde heard there were long-coated men with somber faces asking about him all over town. He confessed to Bonnie that they were possibly policemen wanting him for past crimes, especially within Waco County. He might have to leave town, he said, but would send her a post card notifying her of his whereabouts. She promised to wait for him, as long as it took.

Clyde Barrow

That evening, while packing, Clyde was arrested. He was moved to Waco County for trial and sat out his days and nights in the prisoner ward of the gothic Waco Courthouse awaiting trial. His new-found inamorata, Bonnie, found herself yearning to be near him in letters she penned she called him "Sugar but, Waco seemed like the other end of the world. Finally, against her mother's wishes, she took time off from her job and grabbed a bus to Cousin Mary's house in that city.

During one of her visitations with Clyde, she acquainted his cellmate, Frank Turner, a two-time loser with big dreams. He told Bonnie that because this was third arrest, if found guilty at his upcoming trial he would be sent "up the river for a long time". His only hope was to escape. But, he needed a gun. His parents in East Waco had such an item, and they were out of town. He wondered: If he drew a map of his parents' home, indicating where the gun was stashed, could Bonnie confiscate it and smuggle it in to Clyde? He promised to take Clyde with him.

Bonnie didn't hesitate. She took the blueprint sketched out hurriedly on a napkin by Turner and convinced her cousin to drive straight to East Waco for the treasure hunt. Given the address, the girls broke into the home and followed Turner's directions to where a .32 was concealed in a closet. The next day, while her relative waited in the car, Bonnie carried the weapon in her purse to the visitation dock and slipped it to her Sugar under the noses of the pacing attendants. Clyde then instructed her to go back to Dallas and wait for him.

In court, Frank Turner received the verdict he expected a stiff one: 20 four-year terms for burglary. But, that evening, he and Clyde acted. As a guard slid a tray of supper under their cell bars, Clyde thrust the revolver into his face, simultaneously collaring him. Surprised and frightened, the latter unlocked their cell and mutely took their place inside. Clyde and Turner walked out.

At home, Bonnie had kept constant vigilance on the morning papers. She was delighted to read of the jail break, but when Clyde didn't appear at her door over the next couple of days she understood why. Police sedans were cruising the streets outside Old Man Barrow's gas station. Her absconding Romeo was too hot an item in Dallas to come home now.

Instead, Clyde and Turner absconded to Illinois, robbing service stations, fruit stands and markets along the way. They frequently stole cars to elude the highway patrols. As well, says author E.R. Milner in *The Lives and Times of Bonnie and Clyde*, "Clyde stole automobile license plates and changed them frequently...a practice that he would use extensively later." But, while working mostly Ohio with Turner, Clyde learned an even more valuable lesson in his earliest crime years: to change plates *immediately* after a job. A delay in doing so after robbing a Baltimore & Ohio train depot resulted in his recapture. A passerby had memorized the plate number, notified the police, and the law caught up with him on the road.

Summoned Waco officials returned Clyde and Turner to Texas.

On the road to a crime spree

1932: Early jobs, early murders

Parker poses with cigar and is branded by newspapers as
"Cigar smoking gun moll"
After cops find Joplin film

After Barrow was released from prison in February 1932, he and Ralph Fults assembled a rotating core group of associates and began a series of small robberies, primarily of stores and gas stations; their goal was to collect enough money and firepower to launch a raid of liberation against Eastham prison.

The Barrow gang consists of: Clyde Barrow, Bonnie Parker, Raymond Hamilton, William Daniel "W.D." or "Deacon" Jones, Clyde's brother Marvin "Buck" Barrow and Buck's wife, Blanche Barrow, and Henry Methvin, who came from a large family in northwest Louisiana.

On April 19, Bonnie Parker and Fults were captured in a failed hardware store burglary in Kaufman, Texas, and subsequently jailed. While Parker would be released in a few months, Fults remained in jail and never rejoined the gang.

On the evening of April 30, Clyde and Hamilton awoke the grocer and his wife from bed, demanding that they open the storeroom safe. As Bucher meekly tumbled the lock of the safe, Hamilton's revolver poking his cheek, Clyde stood back with Mrs. Bucher in toe. As Bucher pushed open the iron door of the safe, the edge of it jerked Hamilton's outstretched pistol hand. The gun popped. The grocer grabbed his chest, rattled and fell face downward to the floor. His wife screamed. Again, their task fumbled, the robbers grabbed but a handful of money and escaped.

Ray Hamilton's mug shot

Unlike the Kauffman experience, they couldn't wipe this blunder off as a close call. In the space of a second both men had escalated from thievery to murder, and became wanted fugitives. Tugging the steering wheel to careen around Hillsboro's street corners, finding the nearest way out of town, Clyde pondered what this would mean now to the plans he had for he and Bonnie. Would he ever see her again? And if so, what kind of a life could he offer her on a chronic run?

Mrs. Bucher identified Clyde's and Hamilton's photos from a file of mug shots shown her by the local authorities. State and city police badgered the Barrows for information on their son's whereabouts; their vehicles circled their property night and day.

Little did they realize that Clyde had come and gone, having reached Dallas the night of the murder and having fled shortly thereafter. Admitting to his sister Nell the reason for his flight, he added, "I'm just going on 'til they get me. Then I'm out like Lottie's eye."

He had made a choice and opened the same choice to Bonnie. She could join him or remain behind. The summer months were coming to the Southwest, he asserted, and all that awaited her if she came along would be jumping in and out of stifling autos, hiding in clammy backwoods, and maybe dodging the heat of a hundred roadblocks. He hadn't wanted her implicated thus the reason for his dumping her off in Kauffman but, now he wasn't too blasted sure he could just turn his back on her maybe forever. She responded with a smile and an embrace. She then jotted a message to her mother; and, packing a few minor articles, promised to remain at his side till the end of the road.

Meanwhile, Parker remained in jail until June 17, writing poetry to while away the time. When the Kaufman County grand jury convened, it declined to indict her, and she was released. Within a few weeks, she reunited with Barrow.

Bonnie Is Now Implicated

Long before the end of the road there was a place called Springtown, in Oklahoma, not far over the Red River. Heading as far away from Texas as a night's journey could take them, their stolen Ford sped northbound. As they passed into the outskirts of this town, Bonnie cuddled beside her man in the front seat. In the back were Hamilton and a stray hanger-on pal of Hamilton's, Everett Milligan; both these men drank heavily from a Mason jar full of whiskey. They spotted an open-air community dance in session under colored Chinese lanterns. Its hootenanny fiddles sent Bonnie's toes to tapping.

"I need to shake a leg," Hamilton chuckled, "been in this back seat too long. Let's stop, Clyde. Nuthin's wrong, just wanna dance with a couple pretty things."

Clyde, aware of Hamilton's restlessness, figured that it might do them all a little good to cut loose for maybe a half hour. After all, this hick place looked peaceful enough and there seemed to be no "laws" in sight.

Hardly had the gangsters stepped onto the dance floor when two patrolmen did appear, however, from among one of the clusters of townsfolk. This was August, 1932, and Prohibition was still the law of the land; anyone drinking alcohol was a criminal by virtue of the "Dry Law." The officers, Maxwell and Moore, had spotted the arrival of these latest visitors suspiciously dressed in city clothes and not for a night's hoe-down and had noticed that one of them (Hamilton) seemed to have taken a swig of *something* as he emerged from the car. Now, he seemed to be listing as someone slightly intoxicated. The cops ambled forward to investigate.

"Hey, *you*!" policeman Moore put up a warning palm. "We want to talk to you!"

Both Clyde and Hamilton combusted as only two desperate men wanted for murder would combust. They drew their guns and opened fire at point-blank range. Moore clutched his throat and spun back dead, Maxwell fell over, a wound gaping his stomach.

Everett Milligan was stunned by the others' reaction and when chaos broke loose on the dance floor, he panicked. While Bonnie, Clyde and Hamilton heeled for the getaway car, Milligan blindly groped for an exit in the wrong direction, right into the grasp of a dozen angry men who detained him until the highway patrol arrived on the scene.

Any chance that the killers might not have been identified were scratched when, under duress, Milligan blurted out the names of his accomplices. An all-points bulletin was issued for the apprehension of what the law now called (probably citing Milligan's own words) "The Barrow Gang." Of the two policemen, Maxwell and Moore, the former survived emergency surgery, but the other had died on the spot. The blood of an Oklahoma policeman now on his hands, Clyde decided to quit the state. He raced west.

Bonnie, as clearly as she could think in the wake of the Springtown confusion, remembered her aunt, Nettie Stamps, who lived alone on a farm near Carlsbad, New Mexico. Bonnie had been there to visit her a couple years back and, as she recalled, the acreage offered seclusion where they could buy time to recuperate and rethink.

By nature, Clyde was a fast driver. Whether being pursued by police or on his way to a picnic, he gunned his autos full throttle to the maximum of 70 miles-per- hour. Outside

Carlsbad, the speeding car caught the attention of policeman Joe Johns. Noticing that its fender bore an out of state license plate a rare thing these days when no one had the money to vacation Johns decided not to pursue but trace the license number through the Division of Highways. As he suspected, he learned that that number had been reported stolen days earlier.

Johns spent the afternoon scouting the area. At last, he drove onto the Stamps property where he indeed spotted the vehicle-in-question idle outside Nettie's home. Odd, he thought. He knew the lady who lived here and had always regarded her as law-abiding. When tapping at her door to inquire, Johns was greeted by the steely blue barrel of Clyde Barrow's .38.

When Nettie had seen Clyde reach under his jacket to withdraw the revolver before answering the door, it was then she realized that Bonnie's visit was more than a social call. Now, from her window, she watched perplexed as niece Bonnie, along with those fellas, forced patrolman Johns into their auto and drove off. She hurriedly telephoned the constabulary.

Days later, Johns still could not be found; the law figured he had been murdered. But, the state rejoiced when he finally called headquarters from San Antonio, Texas, where his kidnappers had released him unharmed. The report he filed would give to the world two names that would, from that point, be plastered across American headlines for many months to come and be riddled into a rat-a-tat-tat posterity. One of the abductors, he claimed, was named Ray Hamilton. The other two had given their names to him with proud boast: Bonnie and Clyde.

It wasn't long before Clyde was involved with criminal activity again, this time recruiting several men, including Ralph Fults, to become what was known as the Barrow gang. After Clyde and Fults had raided a hardware store they later joined up with Bonnie only to be chased at high speed.

Despite Clyde's driving skills they were reduced to stealing mules to navigate the Texas farm country and both Bonnie and Fults were eventually arrested. Clyde escaped. Bonnie claimed that she had been kidnapped by the gang but, despite a grand jury failing to indict her, she spent two months in the Kaufman Jail, Texas. On her release she was soon reunited with Clyde.

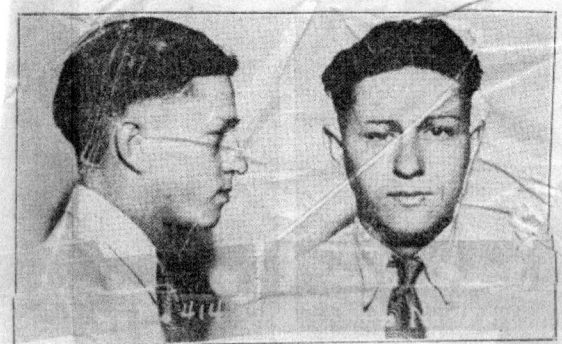

Wanted poster for Clyde Champion Barrow and his brother, Marvin Ivan Barrow. It includes both their physical descriptions and details of their last sighting. The monetary reward of $1000 is the total amount added from the four counties they are wanted in.

Over a considerable period the gang carried out many robberies and kidnappings, some attributed to Bonnie and Clyde.

Their exploits fuelled a mythology that relied on little evidence, but much hearsay and gossip. In some ways the gang were admired as latter day Robin Hoods, while others reviled them as common law breakers. However, it was Clyde's first association with murder that was to garner them greater notoriety.

The Federal Bureau of Investigation (FBI), then called the Bureau of Investigation, became interested in Barrow and his female companion late in December 1932. What was to become the biggest manhunt in the nation at that time started with little understanding of how elusive and tenacious these young criminals were going to turn out to be.

It was while Bonnie was in the Texas jail that Clyde had been identified as the getaway driver during a raid.

If the public had any sympathy or admiration for the Barrow gang, it was quickly dispelled after the shooting and killing of the sheriffs.

He was in such a mood when he and Bonnie robbed the Little Food Store in Sherman, Texas. When proprietor Howard Hill sarcastically smart-mouthed him, Clyde found himself yanking the trigger in anger. Witnesses who had seen the pair emerge from the grocery Clyde's gun barrel still smoking as well as a counter clerk who had stood beside Hall when he fell, all identified the killer.

Bonnie and Clyde were now front-page material, but they rarely stopped in any town long enough to read what was beginning to be their lives' story. For them, it was back in the car and off again on a zig-zag, never-ending auto marathon. The police who pursued found Clyde stealthy and they found him smart. Because he methodically worked many border towns, he was able to pull across the state lines where the local constables couldn't pursue.

Tired of the penny-ante nickel-and-dime stuff that garnered few bucks and another notch in his gun, he decided to hit a few banks. After a roulette of store holdups in and around Carthage, Missouri, where they hid out in a deserted backwoods cabin, Clyde eyed the what-seemed-to-be prosperous Oswego Bank on Nov. 30, 1932. Bonnie had gone in the previous day, pretending to be interested in opening an account, merely to case the layout. She had returned with an excellent description. Now, while Bonnie waited at the wheel, Clyde approached a teller and being none too conspicuous, flashed a .38 in her face and demanded money from her drawer. An alert guard saw the gun and popped a shot at the robber, but missed. Realizing his predicament, Clyde grabbed the only money available in a flash, some $80 lying open at the teller's cage, and left, ducking the shots of the intent but poorly armed guard.

Their first bank job was a failure, but not so much as the small-town bank he chose to stickup the following day. Rushing into its foyer, this time brandishing his guns and yawping like a savage to discourage any would-be guard, he encountered a deserted building. He glowered at the empty teller grids, the desks carpeted with dust and the wall clock that had long quit working, and left in a huff feeling like Fortune's fool.

They returned to Texas to spend Christmas with their families, even if it meant a brief reunion in one of a number of out-of-the-way groves around Dallas. Clyde felt that he needed to add another member to his gang. Since Ray Hamilton had left there had been no one to stand watch while he and Bonnie slept at whatever river bed, back road or orchard they decided to nod a head when they became weary.

Clyde had known the Jones family since childhood and had always considered their boy, William Daniel, a kid with moxie. Quite a few years younger than Clyde, W.D. as he was called noticeably idolized Clyde and now made overtures to join his famous gang. The latter needed to consider Jones was only 16 years old and still somewhat "wet behind the ears" but then again he could handle a car and, being tall and exceedingly muscular for his age, might come in handy if brute force were needed. When Bonnie and Clyde departed Dallas on Christmas Eve, their ranks had risen.

W.D. Jones, photo by gang member

The following day, on Christmas, 1932, Jones' recruitment proved lethal. It was time to steal another car and Clyde figured that W.D. would be good at that after all, he had stolen many in his youth or so he told Clyde. Driving through the little postcard town of Temple, Texas, the gang spotted a new Ford Coupe V-8 parked out front a frame house at 606 S. 13th Street. Having by now driven an assortment of automobiles, Clyde had become a good judge of motor works; he particularly liked the trigger-pin acceleration and roominess of that particular model Ford.

It was broad daylight on 13th Street as Clyde drew up alongside their mark. He instructed W.D. to jump out to see if the keys had been left in the ignition and, if so, he was to follow him and Bonnie out of town where they could transfer their gear from one car to another.

But, the boy was nervous; this being his first assignment for the indomitable Barrow Gang. Nervous fingers could not turn over the car.

"You have to pump the gas!" Clyde yelled. "Just a couple times pump it!"

W.D.'s intermittent attempts to start the motor merely awoke the neighbors who looked out their front windows at the annoying sputter. From his parlor window John Doyle looked out to find strangers berthed in the front seat of his new pride and joy. By this time Clyde had shoved Jones aside and was trying himself to start the auto. The engine flooded, the air reeked of gasoline fumes. Several more sporadic twists of the key finally ignited the buggy. Kicking in, rumbling, the engine calmed and purred.

However, car-owner Doyle had reached the running board. One hand grabbed Clyde by the tie knot, while the other groped for the key from the dashboard. Clyde couldn't shake the aggressor. Residents began spilling onto their front porches, pointing, yelling, accusing. From the other car, Bonnie cried, "Forget about the car, Clyde, leave him alone and let's get out of here!" W.D., not knowing what else to do, sat beside Clyde and whimpered.

Clyde had his gun out and swung to butt his attacker from him, but Doyle in turn grabbed the revolver. In doing so, one finger plucked the sensitive trigger. The weapon roared. Clyde felt the grip on his neck loosen as the other's expression drastically altered. The clumsy angle of the gun had sent a bullet into Doyle's chest. Pushing the now lifeless form onto the curb, Clyde accelerated off 13th Street, Bonnie behind him in the other car. And W.D. still whimpered

W. D. Jones had been a friend of the Barrow family since childhood, and though he was only 16 years old on Christmas Eve 1932, he persuaded Barrow to let him join up with the pair and ride out of Dallas with them that night. The very next day, Jones was initiated into homicide when he and Barrow killed Doyle Johnson, a young family man, in the process of stealing his car in Temple, Texas. Less than two weeks later, on January 6, 1933, Barrow killed Tarrant County Deputy Sheriff Malcolm Davis when he, Parker and Jones wandered into a police trap set for another criminal. The total murdered by the gang since April was now five.

Tarrant County Deputy Sheriff Malcolm Davis-- was felled on the porch of the Lillie McBride house

In evaluating Clyde Barrow's ability to side-step the police and humiliate every roadblock and trap along the thousands of miles of highway he traveled, one must consider the expedient arrest of every accomplice once away from Clyde's uncanny navigation. Ralph Fults was immediately apprehended after the Kauffman, Texas, affair and Ray Hamilton, having bid Clyde an *adieu* to visit his father in Michigan was forthwith taken in that state.

Clyde Barrow fully understood his position. If caught, he would surely die in the electric chair. While this knowledge inspired his sagacity, speed and aggressiveness, it sometimes caused him ill-temper and self-chastisement.

In short, he was beginning to feel weighed down by his crimes. He would often turn darkly irrepressible.

1933: Buck joins the gang

During his incarceration at Huntsville, Buck had managed to jump the walls and made his way across Texas. As a fugitive, he had met and married red-haired Blanche Caldwell. Discovering he was a prison escapee, Blanche convinced him to surrender and "get it all behind".

Ivy "Buck" Barrow, Clyde's brother, with wife Blanche

On March 22, 1933, Buck Barrow was granted a full pardon and released from prison.

Now that he had been paroled she hoped that Buck would consider her father's offer, to help him work his farm. Buck hesitated. "Later, honey," he told her. "I just want to see my baby brother it's been so long." Through his sister Nell (who was kept apprised of Clyde's moves for the benefit of both the Barrow and Parker families), arrangements were made for her brothers to rendezvous in Joplin, Missouri. Buck, with Blanche lit out in late March to find Clyde, ignoring the advice of a friend who told him, "Don't get into that car with him. You'll never come back."

The "Terrible Barrows," not in each other's company since that dismal enterprise in Denton, whooped and hollered it up. The reunion provided an excuse for Clyde and Bonnie to take a desperately needed vacation. Their last several bank jobs had proven lucrative, their pockets jingled, and more importantly, they believed Joplin to be outside the perimeter of the law's concentrated "hunting ground". What better way to relax than by renting a place where the Barrows, together again, could renew acquaintance, share funny stories, play cards, drink and be merry?

Within days, he and his wife, Blanche, had set up housekeeping with Clyde Barrow, Parker and Jones in a temporary hideout at 3347 1/2 Oakridge Drive in Joplin, Missouri. According to family sources, Buck and Blanche were there merely to visit, in an attempt to persuade Clyde to surrender to law enforcement.

Apartment over a double-garage in the quiet Freeman Park

As was common with Bonnie and Clyde, their next brush with the law arose from their generally suspicious—and conspicuous—behavior, not because their identities had been discovered. They chose a well-furnished apartment over a double-garage in the quiet Freeman Park area where they intended to reside for a couple of months before moving on. Neighbors, watching them move in, were alarmed when they spotted a couple of the young men carrying into the flat what appeared to be quite a large arsenal of guns from a car with an out-of-state license plate.

The group ran loud, alcohol-fueled card games late into the night in the quiet neighborhood. "We bought a case of beer a day," Blanche would later recall. The men came and went noisily at all hours, and once, a BAR (Browning Automatic Rifle) discharged in the apartment while Clyde was cleaning it; the short burst did not bring any neighbors directly to the house, but at least one registered suspicions with the Joplin Police Department.

The place was put under surveillance. Police notated that one of two cars a green 1932 Ford Sedan very occasionally left the premises, once in fact on the night of a local bank robbery committed by two men (fitting the Barrows' description) "and a woman." Wiring for information on the Ford's license plates, the cops learned the car had been stolen near Topeka, Kansas, several weeks back.

At mid-morning April 13, Joplin police and county detectives rolled up in front of the garage doors to prohibit any escape with either of the two cars inside. In the flat above, Bonnie was cooking lunch, Clyde was reading the newspaper, W.D. was dozing in the chair and Buck and his wife were engaged in a game. Blanche's small puppy stretched across her lap. It was Clyde who thought he heard something below the window and instinctively peeked through a part in the curtains.

"It's the laws!" he roared, simultaneously lifting his automatic off the sill. Almost as one, he and W.D. fired through the panes at the assemblage of blue uniforms and government-gray overcoats fanning out in the driveway below. County policeman Wesley Harriman and detective Harry McGinnis fell, in direct line of fire. No sooner had their bodies hit the ground than the dozen other lawmen opened up at the upper windows. Glass shards and bullets slammed the ceilings and walls of the apartment, paint and wood chips spraying like rain. Buck had found his shotgun and sent a blast back in return. Bonnie, with a revolver, was sending her own firepower at the assailants. Blanche, at the first sign of action, had screamed and was continuing to scream running blindly from room to room in a paroxysm of panic.

Clyde motioned to the others to head for the garage below, accessible through an interior staircase, while Thompson machine guns continued to turn the fugitives' quarters into hash.

In the garage, Blanche flailed and bawled and, still uncontrollable, broke free from Buck's grasp to run without reason through the back door and out to the lawn. "We'll pick her up!" Clyde grabbed his brother's elbow, and ushered a reluctant Buck into the back seat of the Ford. By the time he slid behind the wheel, and the rest had gathered into the car, he sensed that the laws' volleys had dwindled; it had dawned on them that their shots were no longer being returned and were probably expecting what was to come. Grinning, he turned the ignition and whooped, "Here we come, boys!" loud enough for the laws to hear, then smashed the gas pedal to the floor. Beside him, Bonnie ducked and held onto Clyde's waist. The Ford bolted forward and burst at full speed through the doors. The government's black coupe and the policemen gathered around it all gave way to the force ramming them. Clyde hallooed as the cops spilled across the driveway cursing.

The escapees could see Blanche now, across the street, still running, still screaming, arms still waving. It was the first time Clyde noticed she had her dog tucked into the large pocket of her apron. Bullets whizzing from behind, he braked just long enough for Buck to pick them both up, wife and dog, before speeding west, away from Joplin.

Inside what had once been their apartment, the police found items linking to Bonnie and Clyde photographs of the couple taken with one of those new box Kodak cameras, as well as wanted posters and snipped newspaper headlines they had saved as trophies as part of their brag collection.

But, the identity of that other couple had been a mystery until now. Remaining behind, covered with sawdust and broken glass, were Blanche's purse and Bucks' parole papers.

Warrants on Parker

Different and disparate sources have cited five occasions when Bonnie Parker may or may not have fired shots during crises faced by the gang. The number of shots is unimportant as she never hit anyone, let alone directly murdered. She was, however, an accomplice to 100 or more felony criminal actions during her two-year career in crime including eight murders, seven kidnappings, half-a-dozen bank robberies, scores of felony armed robberies, countless automobile thefts, one major jailbreak and an episode of assault and battery at a time when being a "habitual criminal" was a capital offense in Texas. Because of their far-flung, rural base of operations and will o' the wisp *modus operandi*, Parker was able to stay a step ahead of the tide of legal entanglements that inevitably follow a crime spree the scope of hers and Barrow's.

This began to change for Parker after Joplin: the Joplin Police Department issued a *Wanted for Murder* poster in April 1933 that featured her name and photo first, before Barrow's, though the text concentrated on him. In June, another *Wanted for Murder* poster emerged, this one out of Crawford County, Arkansas, again with Parker's name and photo getting first billing. There was now a $250 cash bounty attached for either of the "Barrow Brothers" (Clyde and "Melvin")—and the admonition to "inquire of your doctors if they have been called to treat a woman that has been burned in a car wreck."

"Barrow Gang" Wanted Poster, 1933 - Van Buren, Arkansas

For the next three months, they ranged from Texas as far north as Minnesota. In May, they attempted to rob the bank in Lucerne, Indiana and robbed the bank in Okabena, Minnesota.

Previously they had kidnapped Dillard Darby and Sophia Stone at Ruston, Louisiana, in the course of stealing Darby's car; this was one of several incidents between 1932 and 1934 in which they kidnapped lawmen or robbery victims, usually releasing them far from home, sometimes with money to help them return. Stories of these encounters made headlines, but so too did the darker encounters. The Barrow Gang would not hesitate to shoot anyone, lawman or civilian, who got in their way. Other members of the Barrow Gang known or thought to have committed murders included Raymond Hamilton, W.D. Jones, Buck Barrow and Henry Methvin. Eventually, the cold-bloodedness of the killings would not only sour the public perception of the outlaws, but lead directly to their undoing.

While the photos in the papers might have suggested a glamorous lifestyle for the Barrow Gang, in reality they were desperate and discontented, as noted in the account of their life written by Blanche Barrow while she was in jail through the latter 1930s. With their new notoriety came difficulty in the smallest tasks of everyday living. Restaurants and motels became less and less of an option; cooking and bathing became campfire and cold-stream propositions. The unrelieved, round-the-clock proximity of life among two couples, plus a fifth-wheel, in one car gave rise to vicious bickering. So unpleasant did it become that W.D. Jones, who was the actual wheelman in the theft of Dillard Darby's car in late April, used that car to get himself separated from the others—and managed to stay separated throughout May and up until June 8.

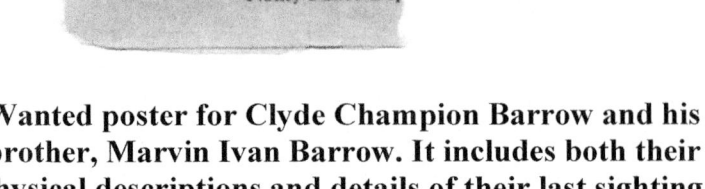

Wanted poster for Clyde Champion Barrow and his brother, Marvin Ivan Barrow. It includes both their physical descriptions and details of their last sighting. The monetary reward of $1000 is the total amount added from the four counties they are wanted in.

Gunning the car down Highway 203 towards Wellington, Clyde was unaware that a bridge over a small gully ahead had been removed for maintenance; none of the gang had noticed the warning sign. Spying the chasm too late, Clyde braked but the car spun, screeched and turned sideways with a jolting thud into the ravine. Bonnie's door threw open and she found herself tumbling from the car, only to have its frame pin her under within seconds. A fire had broken out beneath the hood; miraculously, the rest of the crew, unhurt, yanked her free just as the automobile exploded.

Sources disagree on whether there was an actual gasoline fire or that Parker was doused with acid from the car's battery under the floorboards. What is certain is that Parker sustained serious third degree burns to her right leg. The burn was so severe, the muscles contracted and caused the leg to "draw up". Near the end of her life, Parker could hardly walk and would either hop on her good leg or be carried by Clyde.

One of her thighs was badly burned beneath her tattered dress. Near her knee, the skin was severed to expose bone. She screamed in pain. Tom Pritchard, a nearby farmer who had seen the accident from his field, rushed over to give these "city slickers" a hand and to help carry Bonnie to the family bed. He startled when he noticed revolvers stashed in the men's belts, however. The face of the wounded girl, he realized now, resembled that girl on the wanted poster in the town hall. *What was her name....Bonnie Parker?*

Mrs. Pritchard, in her small way, helped where she could, cleaning the wound and applying iodine. Still, she admitted to Clyde who stood bedside, Bonnie needed a doctor - badly. When Clyde emerged from the bedroom to check on the others, he asked W.D., who sat alone, where everyone had gone. Buck and Blanche, he said, went back to dig the car from the ditch. And the farmer....well, he was out back somewhere, "to tend the animals, I guess." Clyde incensed at Jones' inexperience and searched the property, but could not find Pritchard anywhere. It was obvious, thanks to W.D. who still had a lot to learn, that their host had tiptoed off to a neighbor's house to call the police.

In a dither, the gang was out of there, confusing Mrs. Pritchard who didn't understand the cause of their sudden haste. Clyde had guessed correctly. Taking the Pritchard's car, he was forced to drive miles out of the way to avoid roadblocks that suddenly seemed to grow out of the pavements at every main junction. Managing to find open road again, the gang soon beat the pistons across the Arkansas border. There, they hoped to hide out in the Twin Cities Tourist Camp until Bonnie's condition improved.

Money was scarce, and Bonnie required urgent medical help. Clyde sent W.D. and Buck out by themselves to find quick cash in the encircling area. He remained faithfully with Bonnie, watching her lapse in and out of consciousness until he decided to take a risk and call a doctor from nearby Ft. Smith. When Dr. Eberle arrived, Clyde explained that his "wife had been burned by an exploding oil stove." The doctor did what he could but recommended a hospital or a full-time nurse.

"Barrow hired a nurse," Phillips relates. "In her pain and agony, Bonnie cried continually for her mother. An intensely distraught Clyde fed her, adjusted her pillows, and even carried her to the bathroom." Showing little improvement, Clyde hoped that perhaps the presence of one of her family members would rally her. He called Bonnie's sister, Jean, who rushed up from Dallas.

"Her presence seemed to make a difference," adds Phillips. "Clyde, of course, never left her more than a few minutes. Blanche, too, was a great help. Miraculously, Bonnie began to respond."

On June 23, 1933: Buck and W.D. robbed a bank in Alma and a grocery store in Fayetteville, which resulted in a police chase and a gun battle that killed Marshall Henry Humphreys. (Some sources also say this happened June 26, 1933)

Eventually making their way back to Ft. Smith, they dreaded to tell their leader the bad news of their scrape with the law and the lawman's death.

Clyde drove Jean Parker back to the train and his gang was off again. Luckily, the next car they stole in the relay of never-ending auto thefts had obviously belonged to a doctor; a Gladstone bag in the back seat brimmed with pain killers, wound treatments, gauze, powders and a variety of medicines that allowed Clyde and Blanche to continue to doctor Bonnie's leg. They seemed to be able to keep the gash from festering.

They stole and robbed their way onward, hitting whatever they could to keep their supply of food and money alive. But, the Great Depression had caused these little towns of the Southwest to go bust. The gang needed money and every burgh they hit seemed to provide less and less of the green stuff.

Buck was grouchy and Blanche jumped at the slightest sound. W.D. complained constantly of being hungry. Clyde, who never before seemed to tire at the wheel, was beginning to feel the strain, driving state after state and now back again aimlessly to Missouri. More than anyone, he worried about his little Bonnie, half drugged in the front seat beside him. He recalled the words his sister Nell told him in private at the breakup of the last family rendezvous. Touching his hand with tears in her eyes she had said, "I compare this meeting to some visit with relatives in prison, condemned to die."

Driving silently, forcing himself to keep alert, those words reverberated inside his head as he continued on a northward road toward Platte City.

1933: Platte City and Dexfield Park

Two-unit Red Crown Tourist Court, where the gang's conspicuous behavior drew the police, a gunfight, and a mortal head wound for Buck Barrow.

On July 18, 1933, the gang checked into the Red Crown Tourist Court south of Platte City, Missouri (now within the city limits of Kansas City, Missouri across I-29 from Kansas City International Airport). The Red Crown Court was just two brick cabins joined by garages and the gang rented both. To the south stood the Red Crown Tavern, a popular restaurant and a favorite watering hole for Missouri Highway Patrolmen. Once again, the gang seemed to go out of their way to draw attention to themselves: Owner Neal Houser became interested in the group immediately when Blanche Barrow registered the party as three guests, and Houser, out his rear window, could see *five* people exiting their car—which the driver backed into the garage, "gangster style", for a quick getaway. Blanche paid the lodging tab with coins rather than paper money, and did the same thing again later when she purchased five dinners and five beers for, presumably, three guests. The next day, Houser noticed that his guests had taped newspapers over the windows of their cabin, and Blanche once again paid in silver for five meals. Even Blanche's outfit—tight jodhpur riding breeches —attracted undue attention: they were just not the kind of thing the staid women of Platte City would ever wear, and were the first thing mentioned by eyewitnesses reminiscing even 40 years later. It was all too much for Houser, who brought the conspicuous group to the attention of his restaurant patron, Captain William Baxter of the Highway Patrol.

Crabtree glanced at the index card of important numbers he kept taped below the cash register and dialed the number of the highway patrol. Captain William Baxter, after hearing the clerk's suspicions, promised to check them out. "A bandaged lady," Crabtree had said. Baxter pondered...he recalled that Bonnie Parker was severely injured in an auto accident about a month earlier, then disappeared. Yes, he thought, this made sense, and alerted both his own county forces and the Platte City Police Department.

The following morning, Wednesday, July 19, Clyde hitchhiked into the city, preferring to keep their car in the cabin garage lest the police already had it identified. In town he bought salve, gauze and pills for Bonnie who had been recovering nicely, but still required constant care. (Because a tendon had been injured, she still could not stand well by herself.) The druggist contacted Sheriff Holt Coffey, who put the cabins under watch. Coffey had been alerted by Oklahoma, Texas, and Arkansas to be on the lookout for strangers seeking such supplies. The sheriff contacted Captain Baxter, who called for reinforcements from Kansas City including an armored car.

Clyde arrived back at the Red Crown just after nightfall, tipping his Stetson at the amiable elderly couple who gave him a lift in their flatbed truck. He could see the lights lit through orange curtains in both his and Buck's windows. As assigned, Blanche and W.D. had taken turns watching his Bonnie throughout the day. In the smaller of the two bags he carried were half-dozen cream-filled donuts, Bonnie's favorite kind. The other contained medicines, as well as some food for the crew. Before stepping into his cabin, he noticed, for the first time, what a quiet and pleasant night this was. Tonight, he believed things were looking up.

Before midnight, life would change for Bonnie and Clyde. The very brief life they had left to live. They ran before and had even been scared, but after tonight the couple would drift in an appallingly starker reality than they could handle. What innocence remained in the world would die. If it's true that war changes a person, it changed Bonnie and Clyde. Tonight, hell would break through the limestone to make the gun battle at Joplin look like a water-pistol fight.

Crickets chirruped loudly. And that was about anyone in the tourist camp detected not even the sound of crunching gravel beneath the tires of the armored truck and its convoy of squads that snaked in idle gear onto the grounds. The squads lined up in front of two particular cabins pointed out by the desk clerk, and the armored truck budged in front of the garage doors between the two cabins. It snuffed its engine. When all vehicles were in place, their lights shot on as a unit, one great beam spotting the front-line of cabins.

At 11 p.m. that night, Sheriff Coffey led a group of officers armed with Thompson submachine guns toward the cabins. One policeman banged his flashlight on Buck Barrow's door, loud enough to wake both cabins. "Open up!" is all he said. Blanche's voice sounded frightened within: "You need to wait till I get dressed," she twittered. The policeman then stepped away from the stoop, quickly; he knew what was coming next.

Clyde was already at his window, and realizing their predicament, barked his Browning automatic into the blinding light in front of him. W.D. cut loose with a burst of his machine gun. Next door, Buck, too, was blasting away.

And then it happened: the army of policemen met the gang's defiant shots with a volley that shook the floorboards, a firepower that the bandits had never encountered face-on. They leaped back to avoid the energy that burst apart the window frames and door jams, a barrage that sent plate-size clumps of plaster falling from the ceiling.

But in a pitched gunfight at considerable distances, the submachine guns proved no match for Clyde Barrow's preferred Browning Automatic Rifles, stolen July 7 from the National Guard armory at Enid, Oklahoma.

Obstinate, Buck Barrow attempted to fire back into the onslaught. Stepping too near to his window, two bullets caught his skull. Blood gushed onto Blanche who, behind him, caught him in her arms.

Clyde had picked up Bonnie, fairly well doped with pain killers. Ducking, he kicked open the narrow door that led into the interior of the garage. With W.D.'s help, he laid her in a half-prone position on the back seat. Checking the radiator of their automobile, W.D. was glad to see that bullets hadn't yet penetrated the garage; it was then he caught sight of the armored police vehicle blocking them in.

W.D. knew that the one penetrable item on the monster was, oddly enough, its door. As Clyde carried his maimed brother out to the getaway car, W.D. filled the facing door of the armored van with hundreds of Swiss cheese holes. Inside its cab, the driver dodged ricocheting bullets and caught several in his knees and thighs. In desperation, he reared the vehicle back from the line of fire. And as he did, the Barrow coupe split through the garage doors and into the open courtyard.

As the Barrows laid down withering fire and made their escape, a bullet short-circuited the horn on the armored car and the lawmen mistook it for a cease-fire signal. They did not pursue the retreating Barrow automobile.

Had the police outside been ready, Clyde would have driven into the cannon's mouth. But, because the police couldn't believe this audacity, their trigger fingers stunned long enough to permit Clyde the advantage. He sped directly in front of and past the cordon. At the edges of the driveway, several detectives were ready, aimed, and they fired. The back window of the fleeing auto shattered, one bullet striking W.D.'s shoulder. From the side, even while Clyde veered to avoid them, another group of plainclothesmen got off a couple of final shots, one that obliterated the window nearest Blanche. Stooped over her dying husband to protect him from further harm, a shard of glass pierced her right eye. "I'm blind!" she screamed, and the police heard her wailing as the Barrows roared into the night, much worse for wear.

Buck was dying and Blanche was blinded. W.D. shivered with a chill, having lost blood, and wept. Bonnie moaned, seeming to be having bad dreams. Clyde couldn't go on like this. Driving hours out of Platte City, he pulled aside along the dark country highway and instructed W.D. to steal an automobile parked in the driveway of a set-back farm house. That done, the two cars, their lights out, turned into the next turnoff they encountered Dexfield Park on the Middle Raccoon River, a natural forest preserve where they could at least get a little water.

The Barrows laid down withering fire and made their escape when a bullet short-circuited the horn on the armored car and the lawmen mistook it for a cease-fire signal. They did not pursue the retreating Barrow automobile. Although the gang evaded law enforcement once again, Buck Barrow had sustained a horrific through-and-through bullet wound to the side of the head and Blanche Barrow was nearly blinded from glass fragments in both her eyes. Their prospects for holding out against the ensuing manhunt dwindled.

Buck Barrow mortally wounded with wife Blanche

Back at the Red Crown, the police were licking their minor wounds, considering. Deputy Highfill, the armored car driver, had taken buckshot, but would live; a Sergeant Coffey had a neck wound; his son Clarence (also a lawman) was struck in the elbow. But they were already regrouping and driving off in organized manhunts. They knew they had made pincushions of the gang members.

In the first light of dawn, Clyde could see how bad his brother's injury was. Part of the forehead was blown away under a mass of coagulating blood. Buck stammered, rambling on about things that made no sense. His head lay in the lap of his wife, Blanche, who wore his pair of tinted sunshades to keep whatever light she could from her stinging eye. W.D. had cleansed his wound and had applied a makeshift tourniquet that Bonnie made for him. Much better physically this morning than her fellow fugitives, Bonnie repaid their kindness to her by dressing their wounds, feeding them, and offering words of encouragement. More than all, she refused to let them see that she was frightened, really frightened.

Five days later, on July 24, the Barrow Gang was camped at Dexfield Park, an abandoned amusement park near Dexter, Iowa. Buck's head wound was so severe that Clyde and Jones dug a grave for him. After their bloody bandages were noticed by local citizens, it was determined that the campers were the Barrow gang. Surrounded by local lawmen and approximately one hundred spectators, the Barrows once again found themselves under fire.

Not long after sunrise, Bonnie caught sight of movement in the brush which encircled the clearing. "Clyde," she called out, "it's them *again*!"

Blanche & Buck Barrow

The gang managed to get into the nearest car, the one they had had at the tourist camp, but every path wheelman Clyde tried to take from the clearing was blocked by smoking squirrel rifles. One huntsman hit his mark, Clyde, who caught a bullet in the arm; the car sped out of control and smashed into a tree. The gang stumbled out. Bonnie felt a bullet tear her arm muscle. W.D. wobbled when one grazed his cranium. Finding that their other escape car had been shot apart doors blown off the hinges, tires flattened, grillwork issuing a volcano of steam they had no alternative but to run into the greenwood. They were unable to reach Buck and Blanche who had spilled from the other side of the car upon impact, and cowered, huddled together under a hail of bullets overhead.

Clyde Barrow, Parker, and W.D. Jones escaped on foot by swimming across a river. Buck was shot again, in the back, and he and his wife were captured by the officers. Buck died five days later, at Kings Daughters Hospital in Perry, Iowa, of pneumonia after surgery. Circumstantial Blanche would receive ten years in a women's prison.

Bonnie and Clyde remained on the loose. They wandered the rest of that day through cornfields, nursing their wounds, hiding in barns, eating orchard fruit, until Clyde was able to steal another car.

W.D., lost in the ruckus at Dexfield Park, made no attempt to find his company. He had had enough of fame and glory.

With Buck mortally wounded nearby, Blanche is captured by posse at Dexfield Park, Iowa

Jones's "confession" after his capture sparked murder warrants against the gang

For the next six weeks, the remaining trio ranged far afield of their usual area of operations—west to Colorado, north to Minnesota, and southeast to Mississippi— keeping a low profile and pulling only small robberies for daily-bread money. They restocked their arsenal when Barrow and Jones burglarized an armory at Plattville, Illinois on August 20, acquiring three BARs, handguns, and a large quantity of ammunition.

By early September, they risked a run back to Dallas to see their families for the first time in four months, and Jones parted company with them, continuing on to Houston, where his mother had moved. He was arrested there without incident on November 16 and returned to Dallas. Through the autumn, Barrow executed a series of small-time robberies with a series of small-time local accomplices while his family and Parker's attended to her considerable medical needs.

On November 22, 1933, they again narrowly evaded arrest while attempting to hook up with family members near Sowers, Texas. This time it was their hometown sheriff, Dallas's Smoot Schmid, and his squad, deputies Bob Alcorn and Ted Hinton, lying in wait nearby. As Barrow drove up, he sensed a trap and drove right past his family's car, at which point Schmid and his deputies stood up and opened fire with machine guns and a BAR. The family members in the crossfire were not hit, but a single bullet from the BAR passed through the car, striking the legs of both Barrow and Parker. They escaped that night.

By November 1933, W.D. Jones was in custody and supplying details of the gang's 1933 activities—details which led to the empanelment of a grand jury in Dallas. On November 28, the grand jury indicted Parker, Barrow, and Jones for the murder of Deputy Malcolm Davis in January; Judge Nolan G. Williams of Criminal District Court No. 2 issued arrest warrants for Parker and Barrow for murder. Parker's assistance in the raid on Eastham prison in January 1934 earned her the enmity of an even wider group of influential Texans, so when an eyewitness, later completely discredited, linked her to the heinous Grapevine murders, the head of the Highway Patrol, and the Governor herself, placed bounties on Parker's head.

Just five days later, Barrow and Henry Methvin killed Constable Campbell in Commerce, Oklahoma, and the murder warrant issued there named "Clyde Barrow, Bonnie Parker and John Doe" as his killers.

HENRY METHVIN.
Age 20 (1931). Ht 5-9½ Wt 170. Hair Lt.brown Eyes blue. Complex Fair. Marks and Scars. 1 dim horizontal cut scar left middle finger 1st joint 2 dagger pierced and lettered "love" right forearm inner.

Henry Methvin joined the gang after the Eastham breakout; he and his father, Ivy, ultimately proved its undoing.

Back-tracking, the crew drove exhaustedly into Texas by week's end. They holed up, licking their wounds, in a country motel near Amarillo. For the first time, the Barrow Gang felt hemmed in. What had occurred in Joplin had been *too close* of a call. While Bonnie and Clyde learned from their mistakes, they were smart enough to know: *so had the police*. Clyde had had some trouble clearing Joplin, having taken a few dead ends. From now on he would contrive an escape route *ahead of time*. And although they changed cars and license plates quite frequently, he resolved to do it even more frequently. He accounted that the stolen car he had driven in Joplin might have led the police to them.

Driving into sleepy Ruston, Texas, in early May, they stole a sleek black Chevrolet parked on Trenton Street.

Again, as in Temple, the streets were day lit and again its owner, this time H. Darby Dillard had seen them. As they pulled away, he shouted obscenities from the screened porch of the boarding house where he resided.

Maybe because he was an undertaker, Dillard was not a man to fear death. He convinced a fellow boarder, Sophie Stone, to let him use her auto to pursue the thieves. In the rush of the moment she agreed and found herself tagging along. After momentarily losing sight of his car, Dillard saw it again a few blocks away at a stoplight, W.D. at the wheel. Sliding closer, the forlorn undertaker failed to notice the rest of the Barrows in their original car behind him. They had been following the stolen car to a prescribed junction on the outskirts of town.

Bonnie chuckled, watching Dillard shake his fists violently at W.D. as he edged closer; unaware of the hornet's nest he was being suckered into. At the pre-arranged location, in a less-traveled area, W.D. halted and got out of the car. Seeing this, Dillard braced for fisticuffs. "I'll show him a thing or two," he told Sophie. But, it was then he noticed the reinforcements rolling up behind, their faces crinkled in grins.

Waving his revolver, Clyde stuffed the distraught couple into the back of Dillard's car, which was now the gang's car, between a sullen Buck and W.D. "We're the Barrow Gang," Bonnie told them in a tone not unlike that of a welcoming neighbor, then giggled when her captives' eyebrows elevated.

The curious company drove all night, stopping only to grab some hamburgers, to which they treated their "guests".

Tensions eased and Dillard slowly began to realize that they might not be as bad as the newspapers painted; in fact, even though they dropped him off miles from his home the next morning they slipped him and Stone money to get home. Of course, they kept the car.

1934: Final run

On January 16, 1934, Barrow finally made his long-contemplated move against the Texas Department of Corrections as he orchestrated the escape of Raymond Hamilton, Henry Methvin and several others in the infamous "Eastham Breakout" of 1934. The Texas prison system received national negative publicity from the brazen raid, and Barrow appeared to have achieved what Phillips describes as the burning passion in his life: exacting revenge on the Texas Department of Corrections.

During the jailbreak, escapee Joe Palmer shot prison officer Major Joe Crowson and this act would eventually bring the full power of the Texas and federal governments to bear on the manhunt for Barrow and Parker. As Crowson struggled for life, prison chief Lee Simmons reportedly promised him that all persons involved in the breakout would be hunted down and killed, and all were, except for Henry Methvin, whose life would eventually be exchanged for turning Barrow and Parker over to authorities.

On April 1, 1934, Easter Sunday, Barrow and Henry Methvin killed two young highway patrolmen, H. D. Murphy and Edward Bryant Wheeler, at the intersection of Route 114 and Dove Road near Grapevine, Texas (now the neighboring city of Southlake). A contemporary eyewitness account stated that Barrow and Parker fired the fatal shots and this story got widespread coverage in the press before it was discredited. Henry Methvin later admitted he fired the first shot, after assuming Barrow wanted the officers killed; he also admitted that Parker approached the dying officers intending to *help* them, not to administer the *coup de grâce* the discredited eyewitness had described. Barrow then joined in, firing at Patrolman Murphy.

Most likely, Parker was asleep in the back seat when Methvin started shooting and took no part in the assault.

Placard seen in lower left, marks where the patrolmen's bodies had fallen.
Crowds gathering at the site of the Grapevine ambush, following the incident.
The J.E. Foust Funeral Home of Grapevine, Texas responded to the death scene.

Facing uphill at site of killings (years later)

1934 reenactment facing downhill at site of killings

The Grapevine Murders, Took Place at the Crest of This Hill-- On the Far Side of the Road

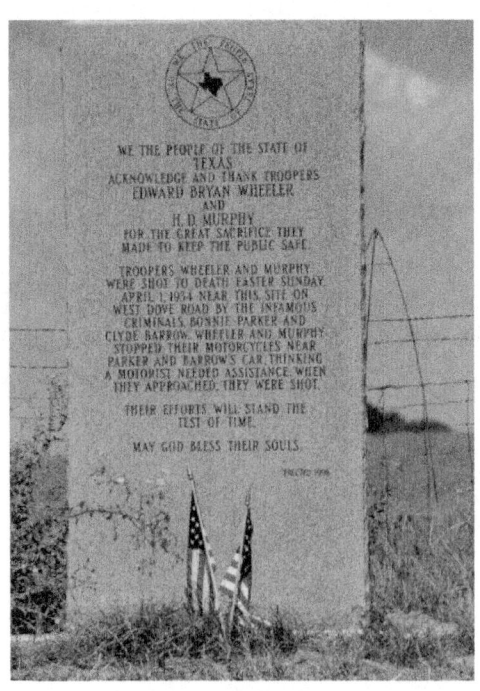

E.B. WHEELER - H.D. MURPHY

Public tide turned against the couple after the Grapevine murders and resultant publicity

In early April 1934, a stolen car was found abandoned in Kansas and linked to Barrow through a bloody fingerprint. The car, it later was determined, had been stolen early March 31 from Shreveport businessman Philip Bloomer, who lived in South Highlands. Barrow used the car in the slaying highway patrolmen, H. D. Murphy and Edward Bryant Wheeler.

"The car was stolen from Bloomer's driveway, but no one knew until later that Bonnie and Clyde had stolen it, so nothing (was) in the news," Shreveport historian Eric J. Brock said. "Police records show that it was stolen that date and later ditched in Kansas when they stole the car that became the death car. That is when the authorities put two and two together and realized who had taken the Bloomer car."

Public hostility only increased when, five days later, Barrow and Methvin killed 60-year-old Constable William "Cal" Campbell, a widower single father, near Commerce, Oklahoma. They kidnapped Commerce police chief Percy Boyd, drove around with him, crossing the state line into Kansas, and then let him out with a clean shirt, a few dollars and a request from Parker to tell the world she did not smoke cigars. The outlaws did not realize at their upbeat parting that Boyd would identify both Barrow and Parker to authorities—he never learned the name of the sullen youth who was with them—and when the resultant arrest warrant was issued for the Campbell murder, it specified "Clyde Barrow, Bonnie Parker and John Doe." Historian Knight writes: "For the first time, Bonnie was seen as a killer, actually pulling the trigger—just like Clyde. Whatever chance she had for clemency had just been reduced."

April 1934, The Texas Department of Corrections then contacted former Texas Ranger Captain Frank A. Hamer, and persuaded him to accept an assignment to hunt down the Barrow Gang. Though retired, Hamer had retained his commission, which had not yet expired. He accepted the assignment as a Texas Highway Patrol officer, secondarily assigned to the prison system as a special investigator, and given the specific task of hunting down Bonnie, Clyde and the Barrow Gang.

Former Texas Ranger Frank Hamer

Former Texas Ranger Frank Hamer became the Barrow Gang's relentless shadow after the embarrassing Eastham prison breakout.

Tall, burly, cryptic and taciturn, unimpressed by authority, driven by an "inflexible adherence to right, or what he thinks is right," for twenty years Hamer had been feared and admired throughout the Lone Star State as "the walking embodiment of the 'One Riot, One Ranger' ethos."

In accomplishing the aims of Texas law enforcement he "had acquired a formidable reputation as a result of several spectacular captures and the shooting of a number of Texas criminals." He was officially credited with fifty-three kills (and seventeen wounds to himself). Although prison boss Simmons always said publicly that Hamer had been his first choice for the Barrow hunt, there's evidence he approached two other Rangers first, both of whom had been queasy about shooting a woman and declined; Hamer apparently had no such qualms. Starting February 10, he became the constant shadow of Barrow and Parker, living out of his car, just a town or two behind the bandits. Three of Hamer's brothers were also Texas Rangers, and while brother Harrison was the best shot of the four, Frank was considered the most tenacious.

In the spring of 1934, the reality of the Grapevine killings had far less impact on events than did the public's perception of them: All four Dallas daily papers seized on the story told by the eyewitness, a farmer, who claimed to have seen Parker throw her head back and laugh at the way Patrolman Murphy's head "bounced like a rubber ball" on the ground as she pumped bullets into his prone body. The stories even claimed that police found a cigar butt "with tiny teeth marks" that could only be attributed to the diminutive Parker. Things got worse several days later when Murphy's intended bride walked into his funeral wearing her wedding gown and sparked another round of photo-supported coverage in the papers. The eyewitness's ever-changing story was soon discredited, but not in time for Barrow and Parker: the massive negative publicity, against Parker in particular, accelerated the public clamor for the extermination of the remaining elements of the Barrow Gang.

It was more than just bad press, though—the outcry galvanized the authorities into taking more concrete legal actions. Highway Patrol boss L.G. Phares immediately offered a $1,000 reward for "the dead bodies of the Grapevine slayers"—not their capture, just the bodies. Texas governor Ma Ferguson was as outraged as the voting public, and added another $500 reward for each of the two alleged killers, which "meant for the first time there was a specific price on Bonnie's head, since she was so widely believed to have shot H.D. Murphy."

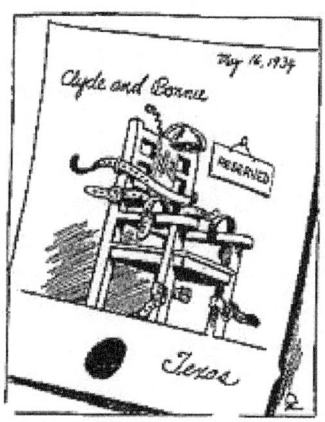

The Dallas Journal ran a cartoon on its editorial page showing the Texas electric chair, empty, but with a sign on it saying *"Reserved"—for Clyde and Bonnie.*

The End of the Ride

It was a season of "lasts." On May 6, Bonnie and Clyde met with their families for what would be the last time on a rural road near Dallas. Solemnity weighted the air. Everyone felt it. And none avoided it, especially Bonnie who alluded to a forthcoming death. When her mother asked Bonnie not to talk about death, Bonnie hugged her and, according to *The Lives and Times of Bonnie and Clyde*, replied, "Now Mama, don't get upset...It's coming. You know it. I know it...Mama, when they kill us, don't ever say anything ugly about Clyde." She then handed her a poem she had written, which she called simply, *The Story of Bonnie and Clyde*. This poem, which her mother had printed in the newspapers, is a remarkable piece of self-realization from a woman whose understanding of herself, her world and her times provides the reader with the realization that, despite its coarseness, it was written by a very insightful woman.

The Poem

Following is a poem written by Bonnie Parker somewhere in the last weeks of her life: (The punctuation is hers.) She entitled it:

The Story of Bonnie and Clyde

You've read the story of Jesse James
Of how he lived and died
If you're still in need for something to read
Here's the story of Bonnie and Clyde.

Now Bonnie and Clyde are the Barrow gang,
I'm sure you all have read
how they rob and steal
And those who squeal are usually found dying or dead.

There's lots of untruths to those write-ups
They're not so ruthless as that
Their nature is raw, they hate all law
Stool pigeons, spotters, and rats.

They call them cold-blooded killers
They say they are heartless and mean
But I say this with pride, I once knew Clyde
When he was honest and upright and clean.

But the laws fooled around and taking him down
and locking him up in a cell
'Till he said to me, "I'll never be free
So I'll meet a few of them in hell."

The road was so dimly lighted
There were no highway signs to guide

But they made up their minds if all roads were blind
They wouldn't give up 'till they died.

The road gets dimmer and dimmer
Sometimes you can hardly see
But it's fight man to man, and do all you can
For they know they can never be free.

From heartbreak some people have suffered
From weariness some people have died
But all in all, our troubles are small
'Till we get like Bonnie and Clyde.

If a policeman is killed in Dallas
And they have no clue or guide
If they can't find a friend, just wipe the slate clean
And hang it on Bonnie and Clyde.

There's two crimes committed in America
Not accredited to the Barrow Mob
They had no hand in the kidnap demand
Nor the Kansas City Depot job.

A newsboy once said to his buddy
"I wish old Clyde would get jumped
In these hard times we's get a few dimes
If five or six cops would get bumped."

"The police haven't got the report yet
But Clyde called me up today
He said, "Don't start any fights, we aren't
working nights, we're joining the NRA."

From Irving to West Dallas viaduct
Is known as the Great Divide

Where the women are kin and men are men
And they won't stool on Bonnie and Clyde.

If they try to act like citizens
And rent a nice little flat
About the third night they're invited to fight
By a sub-gun's rat-tat-tat.

They don't think they're tough or desperate
They know the law always wins
They've been shot at before, but they do not ignore
That death is the wages of sin.

Someday they'll go down together
And they'll bury them side by side
To few it'll be grief, to the law a relief
But it's death for Bonnie and Clyde.

Henry Methvin

Hamer, in the meantime, had learned of the couple's meeting with their folks in Dallas. He put two and two together and, again, guessed correctly. He presumed that they were probably *en route* next to visit with Methvin's father, Iverson, who lived in Acadia, Louisiana, in the northern part of the state near Shreveport. And that is exactly where the outlaw trio headed.

Ever since the massacre in Grapevine, in which he killed the motorcycle trooper, Henry Methvin was skittish.

He had known from that moment on that he had gotten into something way over his head. And he had heard the "death talk" during the Barrow- Parker reunion; had seen the sullen faces; had read Bonnie's poem which spoke of death. Henry Methvin was not presupposed to the idea of accepting what Bonnie called "the wages of sin". Simply, Henry wanted to live.

By the time they arrived in Shreveport, Methvin was a bundle of nerves. Holing up at Iverson's out-of-the-way cabin off Sailes Road, Henry confessed his fears to his father. While Bonnie and Clyde slept in an adjoining room, he rued his association with them. He wished, he told Iverson, that he could wake up and find himself pardoned of all his crimes and start life anew. This gave Iverson an idea.

When Hamer, Hinton and the other troopers paused in Shreveport on May 19, they felt that the end was near. Hamer contacted Chief of Police Tom Bryan to inform him of their plans for an ambush, but in turn received startling news. Mr. Methvin had paid Bryan a visit offering a deal: *Bonnie and Clyde for a reduced sentence for his son.* Hamer asked to see Iverson Methvin immediately.

Sometime during the day of May 22, final preparations were made for an ambush. The plan that resulted was devilishly simple. Bonnie and Clyde, Methvin confessed, were staying at his cabin. During the day they tended to make early visits to town in nearby Sailes. The Sailes Road was dense with woodland, moss hanging low over the road. The road was narrow and there were plenty of places a posse could wait concealed.

"But, how do we know your son won't be with them?" asked Hamer. That problem, Hamer learned, had already been conveniently worked out by fate. A day earlier Bonnie, Clyde and Henry Methvin had driven to Shreveport for hamburgers; while Methvin went in to order, a police squad had pulled alongside the Barrow car in a parking lot. Clyde, apprehensive with its appearance, calmly pulled away, intending to circle the neighborhood and come back for Methvin later. But, Henry, having noticed what had occurred, left without his order and went into hiding. The couple returned to Iverson's cabin alone, assuring the father that his son would reappear eventually.

Details were worked out. Iverson, a logger by trade, owned a beat-up Model A truck that he occasionally used to haul pulp lumber to Sailes. Clyde often poked fun at the truck, so would recognize it on sight. If Clyde were to spot that truck stalled, say, on Sailes Road, would he not stop to investigate? A handshake and a promise of leniency for Henry Methvin ended the dialogue.

Hinton's account has the group in place by 9:00 pm on the 21st and waiting through the whole next day (May 22) with no sign of the outlaw couple, but other accounts have them setting up on the evening of the 22nd.

The spot that the agents chose for the ambush that next morning, May 23, 1934, was atop one of the many low rolling hills that the road traversed. "Moss-covered trees grew so close to the road at this point that we were hidden from view but we could see anyone approaching for almost a half-mile on the road from either direction," writes Ted Hinton. Old Man Methvin's beater had been parked alongside a small ditch that ran along the north side of the road; the sharpshooters kneeled across the way directly from it.

Iverson himself waited among the posse, biting his fingernails. Joining the posse were County Sheriff Henderson Jordan and Bienville Parish Deputy Prentis Oakley.

Left to right) top row: Ted Hinton, P.M. Oakley, and B.M. Gault, bottom row: Bob Alcorn, Henderson Jordan, and Frank Hamer

Clyde and Bonnie had gone to town at daybreak and unless this day differed from the others, would be passing this point on their way back to the Methvin cabin around 9 a.m. Ted Hinton and Bob Alcorn, who knew Barrow and Parker by sight, were posted nearest the road to avoid gunning down the wrong party. At fifteen minutes past nine Bob Alcorn pointed to a beige '34 Ford approaching from over the nearest hill. As it sped towards them, it seemed to slow down, its driver's eyes on the abandoned truck. The current license plate on the car was an Arkansas one, 15-368.

"This is him," Hinton side-mouthed, and lifted his Browning automatic to his shoulder, the silhouette of Clyde Barrow's head square in its sight. Each of the other officers was equipped with like weapons, loaded with five full rounds. They watched Clyde's form bending forward, scanning the truck, and then twisting sideways to look for its owner among the trees. Body movement bespoke curiosity. Beside him sat Bonnie; wearing a dress of red, her favorite color. Hinton heard Hamer, beside him, clear his throat.

But, Hamer chose not to call out a warning not to Bonnie and Clyde, who always escaped when given even the slightest advantage. There would be no advantage here. Instead in a voice audible only to those around him, void of drama, void of malice, Hamer ordered, "Shoot!

Barrow was killed instantly by Oakley's initial head shot, but Parker had a moment to reflect; Hinton reported hearing her scream as she realized Barrow was dead before the shooting at her began in earnest. The officers emptied the specially ordered automatic rifles, as well as other rifles, shotguns, and pistols at the car, and any one of many wounds would have been fatal to either of the fugitives. According to statements made by Ted Hinton and Bob Alcorn:

"In the book, *Ambush*, Hinton tells the rest: "...Bonnie screams, and I fire and everyone fires...My BAR spits out twenty shots in an instant, and a drumbeat of shells knifes through the steel body of the car, and glass is shattering. For a fleeting instant, the car seems to melt and hang in a kind of eerie and animated suspension, trying to move forward, spitting gravel at the wheels, but unable to break through the shield of withering gunfire...My ears are ringing, there is a spinning and reeling in my head from the cannonade of bullets and the clank of steel-jacketed metal tearing steel...." And when the firing subsided..."Clyde is slumped forward, the back of his head a mat of blood...I scramble over the hood of the car and throw open the door on Bonnie's side. The impression will linger with me from this instant I see her falling out of the opened door, a beautiful and petite young girl...and I smell a light perfume against the burned-cordite smell of gunpowder..."

Although certainly a supporter of Clyde and his gang, by the time of her death, there were no outstanding warrants for Bonnie's arrest alleging murder. There is in fact little reliable evidence that she ever shot anyone, but by the time of her death in 1934, her fate had been inextricably linked with that of her companion Barrows.

The trail ended here on a desolate road, deep in the piney Louisiana woods.

To the right of the road stands a monument marking the location of the shooting.

The memorial today

Their gunfire was so loud, the posse suffered temporary deafness all afternoon

Some today say Bonnie and Clyde were shot more than fifty times, others claim closer to twenty-five wounds per corpse, or fifty total. Officially, the tally in parish coroner Dr. J. L. Wade's 1934 report listed seventeen separate entrance wounds on Barrow's body and twenty-six on Parker's, including several headshots on each, and one that had snapped Barrow's spinal column. So numerous were the bullet holes that undertaker C. F. "Boots" Bailey would have difficulty embalming the bodies because they wouldn't contain the embalming fluid.

Amidst the lingering gun smoke at the ambush site, the temporarily deafened officers inspected the vehicle and discovered an arsenal of weapons including stolen automatic rifles, sawed-off semi-automatic shotguns, assorted handguns, and several thousand rounds of ammunition, along with 15 sets of license plates from various states. Word of the ambush quickly got around when Hamer, Jordan, Oakley, and Hinton drove into town to telephone their respective bosses. A crowd soon gathered at the spot, and Gault and Alcorn, who had been left to guard the bodies, lost control of the jostling curious; one woman cut off bloody locks of Parker's hair and pieces from her dress, which were subsequently sold as souvenirs. Hinton returned to find a man trying to cut off Barrow's trigger finger, and was sickened by what was occurring.

The coroner, arriving on the scene, saw the following: "... nearly everyone had begun collecting souvenirs such as shell casings, slivers of glass from the shattered car windows, and bloody pieces of clothing from the garments of Bonnie and Clyde. One eager man had opened his pocket knife, and was reaching into the car to cut off Clyde's left ear."

The coroner enlisted Hamer for help in controlling the "circus-like atmosphere", and only then did people move away from the car.

The bullet-riddled Ford containing the two bodies was towed to the Conger Furniture Store & funeral parlor in downtown Arcadia, Louisiana. Preliminary embalming was done by Bailey in the small preparation room in back of the furniture store. It was estimated that the northwest Louisiana town swelled in population from 2,000 to 12,000 within hours, the curious throngs arriving by train, horseback, buggy, and plane. Beer which normally sold for 15 cents a bottle jumped to 25 cents; ham sandwiches quickly sold out. After identifying his son's body, an emotional Henry Barrow sat in a rocking chair in the furniture part of the Conger establishment and wept.

"THE DEATH CAR"

Bonnie in the front seat

Officers inspect Clyde Barrow and Bonnie Parker's bullet-riddled V8 Ford at the police impound after removing the couple's bodies. Dallas County Sheriff Smoot Schmid is at left, hatless.

Clyde Barrow (head resting against the door)
Just minutes after the ambush, May 23, 1934

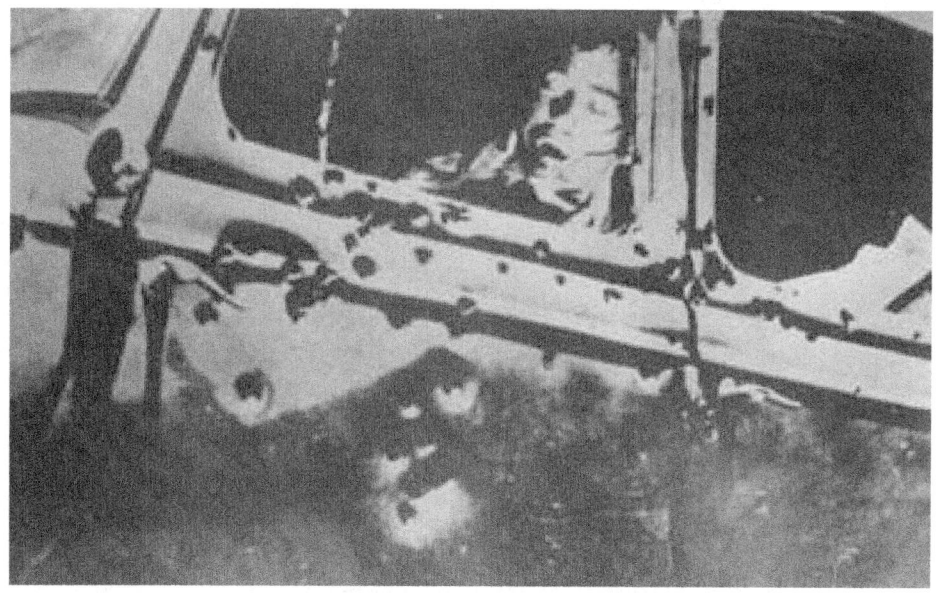

Clyde Barrow (head resting against the door)
Just minutes after the ambush, May 23, 1934
NOTE: it was later determined that this photo may have been a doctored photo.

We will look at some of the other photos to see how it may have been accomplished.

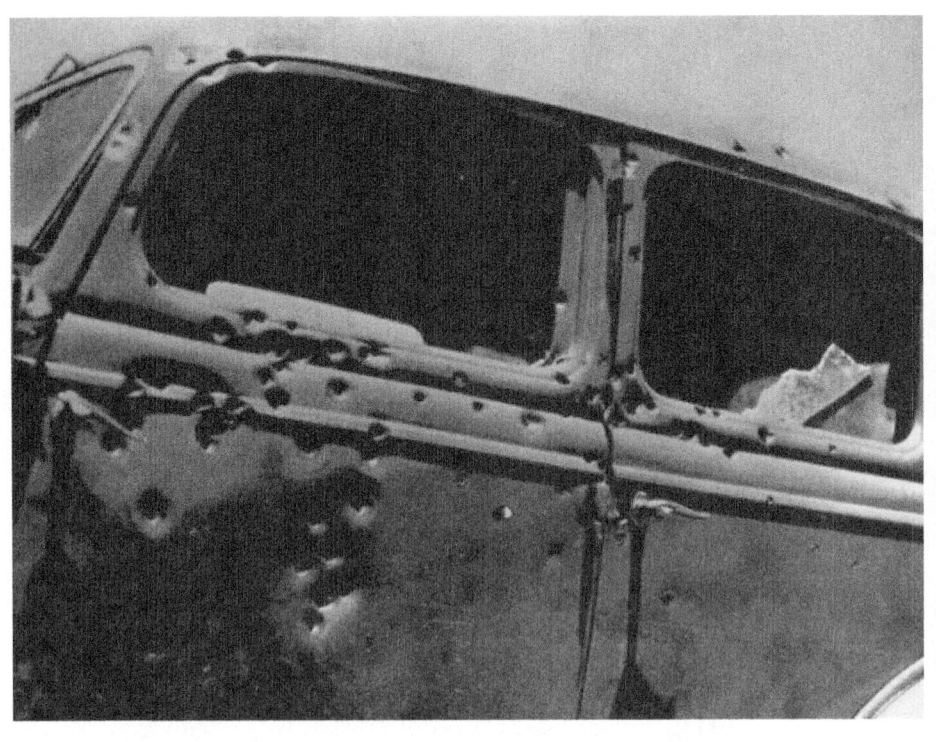

Original photo taken of the death car alone

Original photo of Clyde's body

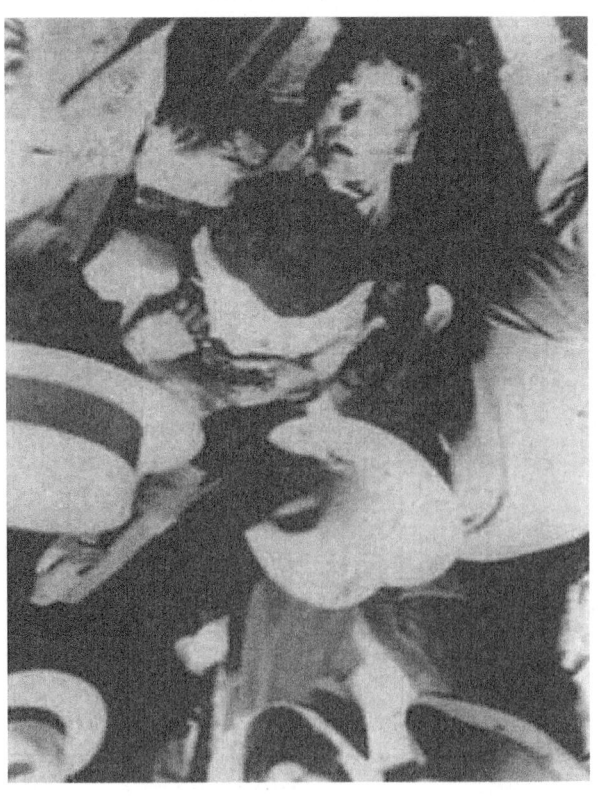

Original photo rotated around (for Clyde's head shot alignment)

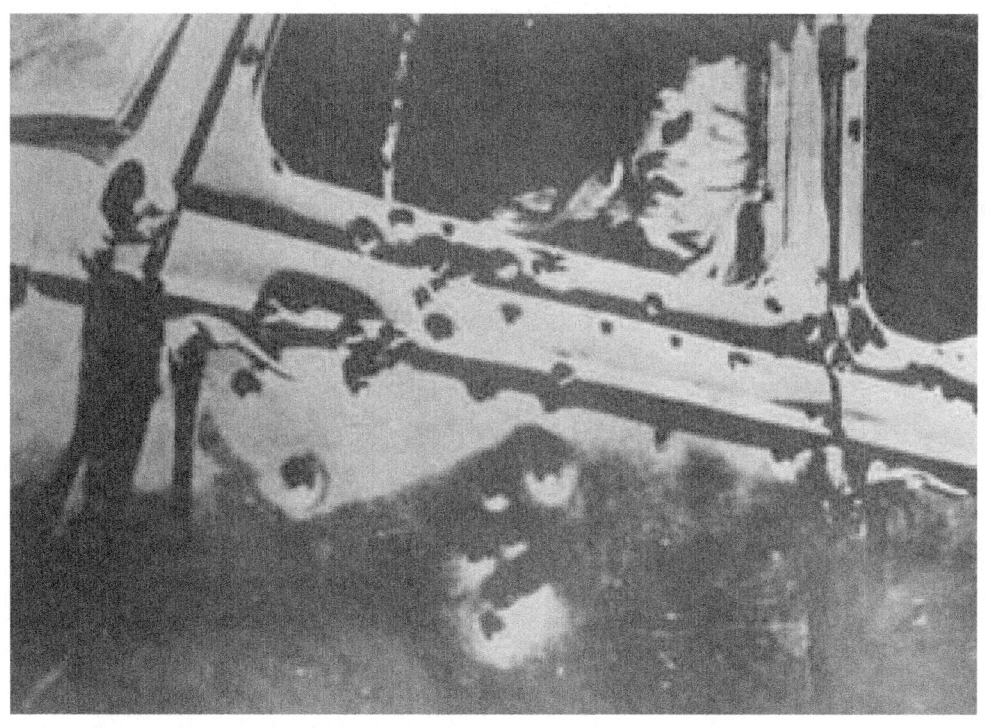

"Doctored" photo of Clyde's body in car is revealed

Just like today, the media alters pictures and bends the truth to sell their news.

Besides the large arsenal of weapons found throughout the car, the lawmen found under the back seat, fifteen license plates from various states

The death car is now on display

167 BULLETS LATER

H.D. Darby, a young undertaker who worked for the McClure Funeral Parlor in nearby Ruston, Louisiana, and Sophia Stone, a home demonstration agent also from Ruston, came to Arcadia to identify the bodies. They had been kidnapped by the Barrow gang the previous year in Ruston, on April 27, 1933, and released near Waldo, Arkansas. Parker reportedly had laughed when she asked Darby his profession and discovered he was an undertaker. She remarked that maybe someday he would be working on her. As it turned out, she could be no closer to the truth: Darby assisted Bailey in embalming the outlaws.

Bodies being removed from death car

Bonnie Parker   Clyde Barrow

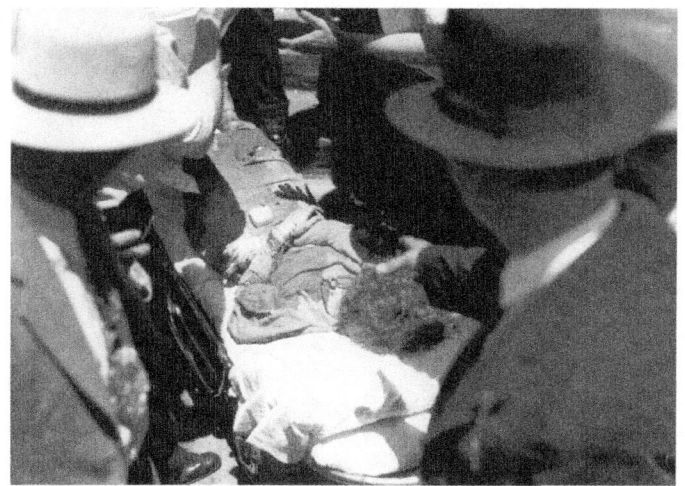

Above photo shows Bonnie's body being removed

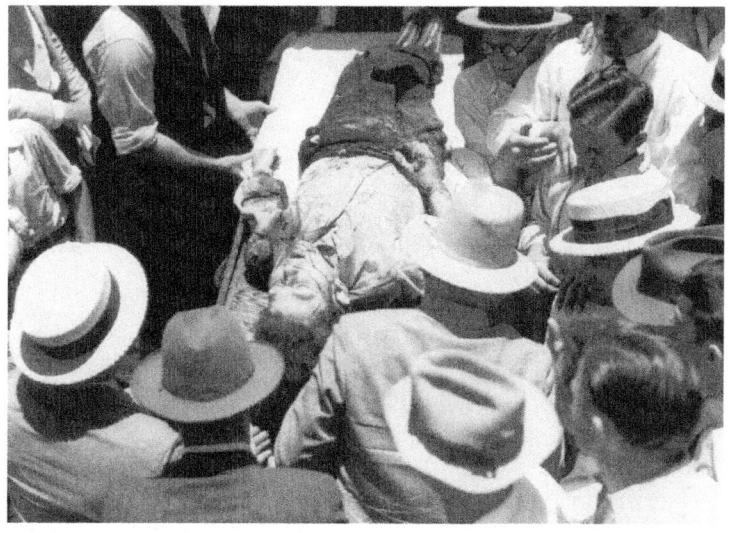

Above photo shows Clyde's body being removed

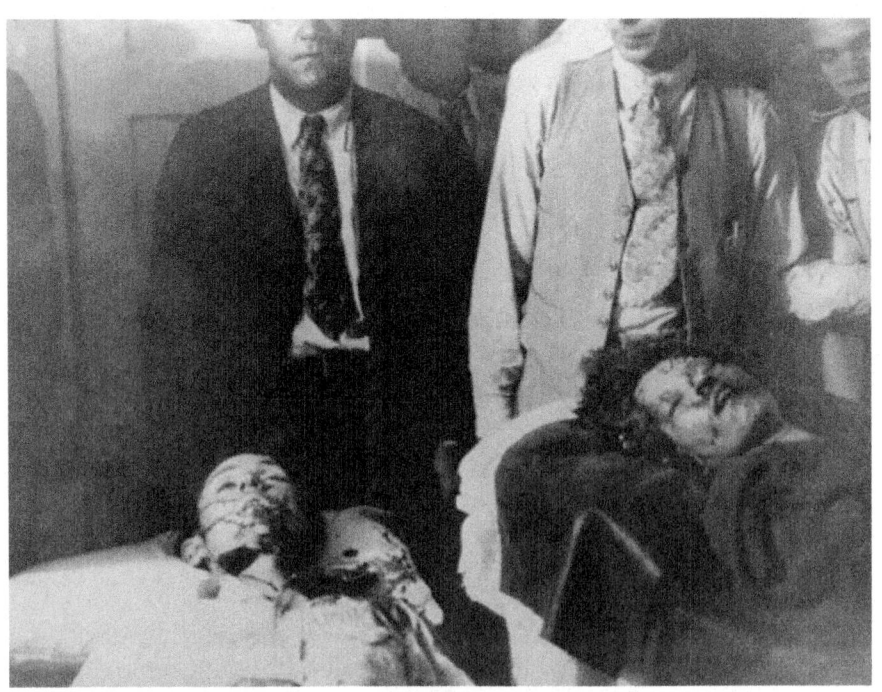

Bodies as they were first brought in.

Bonnie Parker

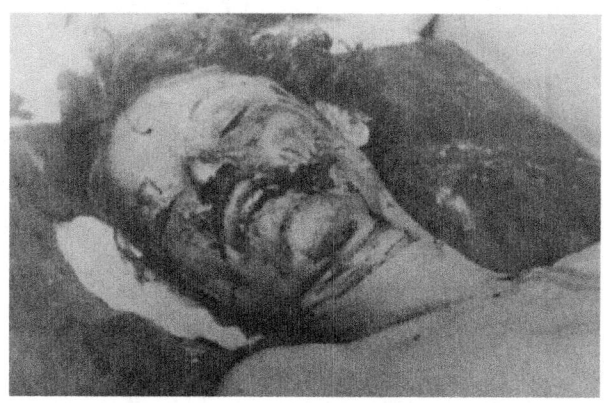

**The body of Bonnie Parker was taken to Conger's Furniture Store and
Funeral Parlor two hours after the ambush near Arcadia, Louisiana.**

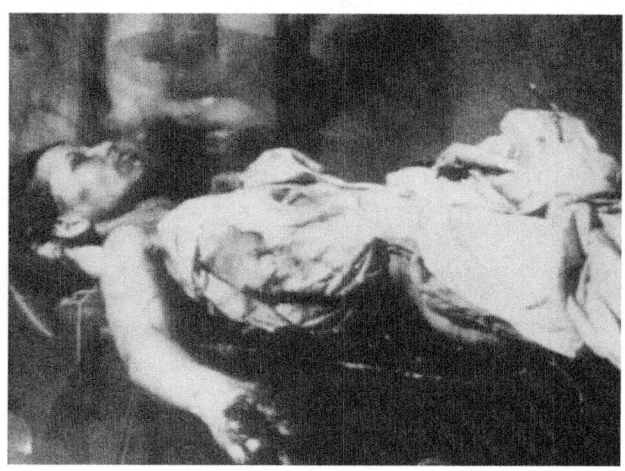

Very eerie image!!!

CLYDE BARROW

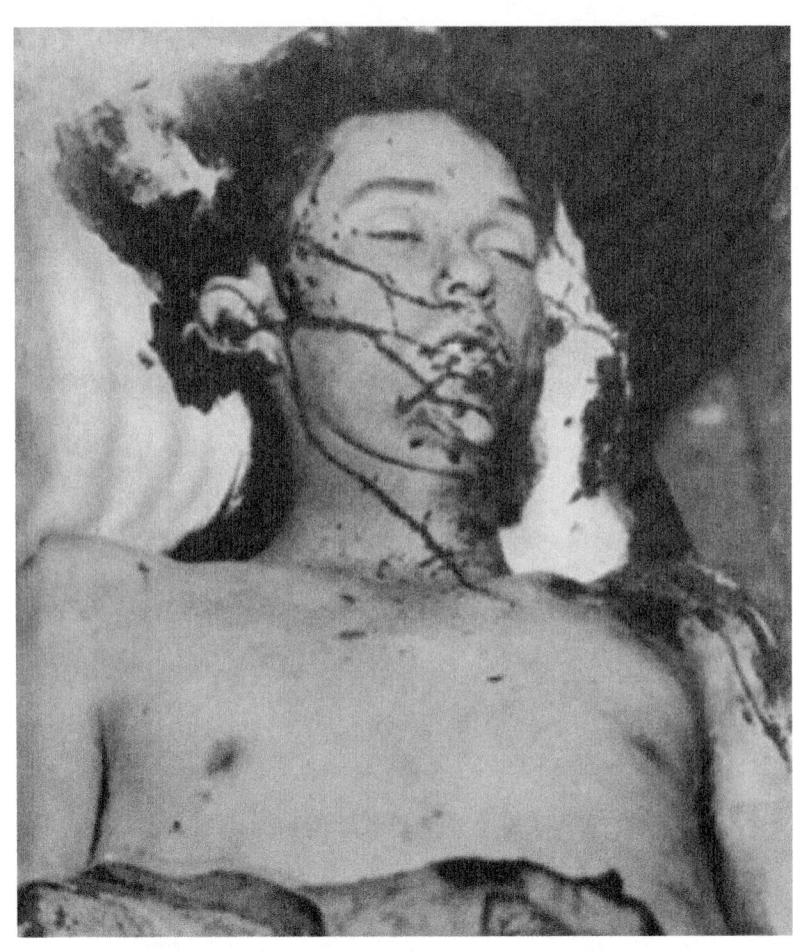

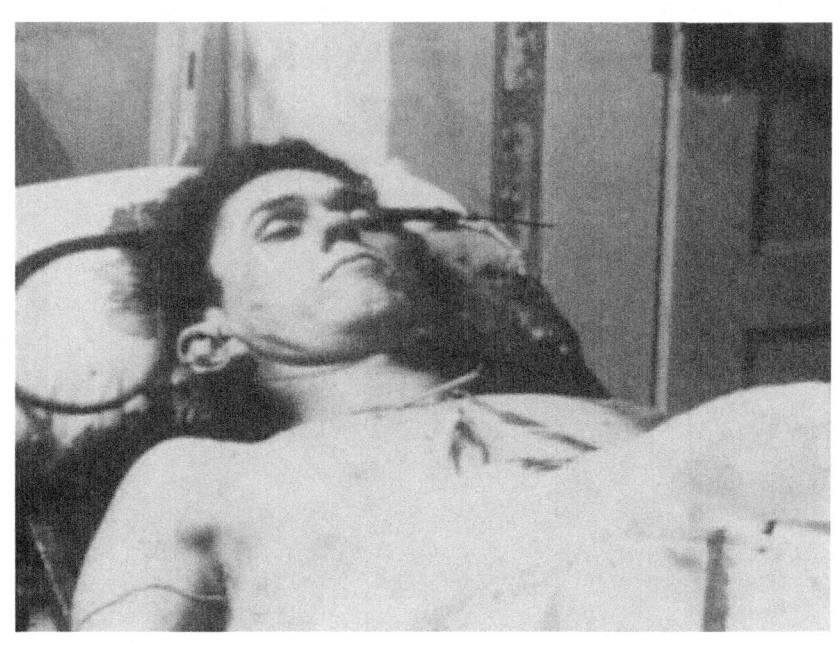

CORONER'S REPORT ON THE BODIES OF
BONNIE PARKER & CLYDE BARROW

DR. J.L. Wade
Medical doctor and coroner
Bienville Parish

BONNIE PARKER

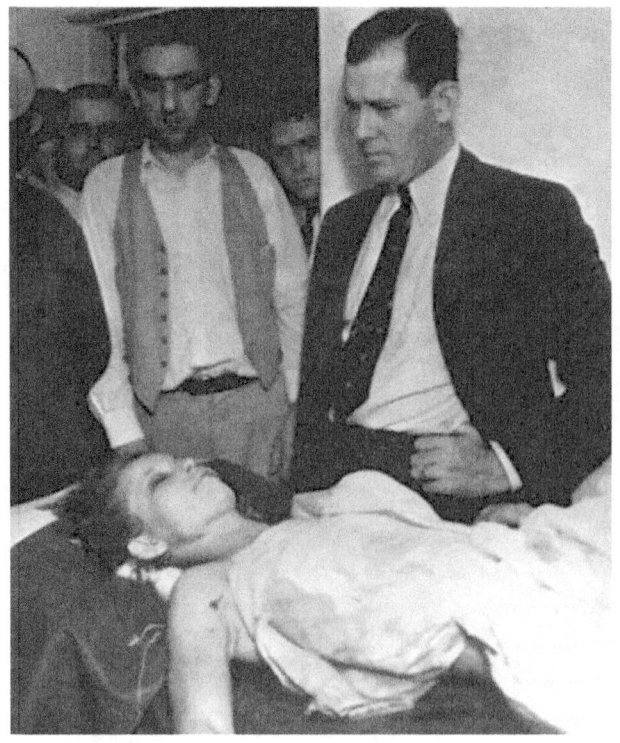

one gold wedding ring on third
finger of left hand

small watch on left arm

a three acorn brooch on dress, in front

one small catholic cross under dress

red dress and red shoes

tattoo of two hearts with arrow, above the
right knee, names Roy on right side, and
Bonnie on the left side

shot in left breast, going into chest

shot 4" below ear

another shot, entering above the right knee

two shots front leg

two shots right leg

gunshot wound around edge of hair, 1 1/2" above the left ear

another through the mouth on left side, exiting at top of jaw

another at middle, just below left jaw

another above clavicle, left side, going into the neck

another entering chest 2" below the inner side of left shoulder

two shots about 2" below left shoulder, fracturing the bone

another wound on elbow of left arm

another entering left chest above the heart, breaking ribs

six shots entering 3" on back region left side

five pellet wounds about the middle of left side

cuts from glass on the left ankle

cut on top of left foot, apparently from glass

cut on center of right thigh

cut 6" in length, about 3 1/2" center of right leg

eight metal fragments centering across the front of face

exit wounds 6" on the inner side of right leg

flesh wound underside of right knee

bullet wound right leg about middle of outer right knee

wound on center of ankle about 2" above back of foot

gunshot wound to bone of first finger

another to the middle finger

gunshot wound entering fleshy portion of left thigh

eight bullet wounds striking almost in parallel line on left side

three parallel lines of bullets striking right side of back from base of neck to angular right capular to middle of back bone, one striking midway of back, breaking backbone

note: Although not in the coroner's report, it was rumored at the time, that Bonnie was

two and a half months pregnant when killed.

CLYDE CHESTNUT BARROW

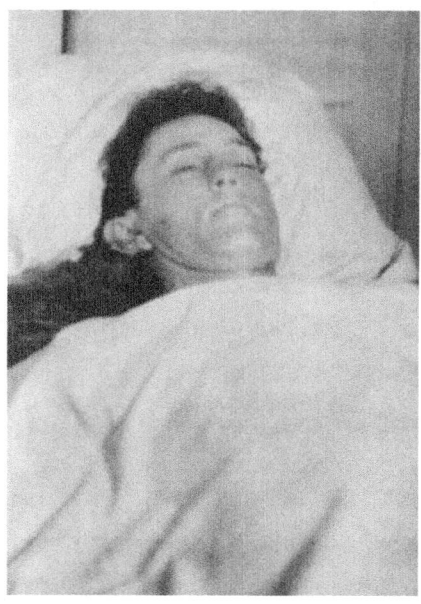

on the right arm, tattoo picture of girl
under which is written Grace

on the inner side, an anchor and shield
with initials "USN"

on the left forearm, a dagger through a
heart and the initials "E.B.W."

on left shoulder, a rose and leaves

gunshot wound in head, center front of left
ear, exiting about 2" above right ear

one entering edge of brain above left eye

several shots entering left shoulder joint

small glass cut at joint, first finger of

right hand

seven small bullet wounds around middle of
right knee

a number of glass wounds
bullet wound right leg, about middle of outer
left knee

bullet wound on exterior ankle

wounds about face

wound 2" above back, a great hole

gunshot wound, back of first finger.

another wound, middle finger at bone,

severing the member

The Aftermath

By today's standards such an incident would precipitate an investigation, particularly when a maverick law enforcer such as Hamer clearly took the law into his own hands. Despite having been no warrants against Bonnie to justify killing her, Hamer and the Louisiana authorities had decided that execution was the preferred option.

Whatever the view of such an act from a moral perspective, what certainly was questionable behavior by Hamer and some of his posse was to keep several of the stolen guns found in Bonnie and Clyde's car as souvenirs and then later sell them.

In the town of Gibsland, Louisiana a 'Bonnie & Clyde Festival' is held every year on Highway 154 on the anniversary of their deaths. Sadly the innocent victims of the Barrow gang, which number around 34, are not remembered with the same degree of idolatry.

Along with ghoulish memorabilia, a romanticized Oscar winning movie and even a poem by Bonnie herself published for the world to read, the mythology of the two illiterate, cold-hearted criminals, continues unabated.

Funeral and burial

PARKER FUNERAL

Deaths and Funeral Notices

PARKER.—Bonnie, age 22, died Wednesday at Arcadia, La. Survived by her mother, Mrs. Emma Parker; one sister, Mrs. Billie Mace, and brother, Hubert Parker. Funeral services will be held at McKamey-Campbell Funeral Home, 1921 Forest, at 2 p. m. Saturday, also private services at the grave.

Crowds gather outside of Conger's Furniture Store and Funeral Parlor

Photograph of a large crowd outside of the McKamy Campbell Funeral Home present for Bonnie Parker's funeral.

This is a picture of how many people attended Bonnie's funeral

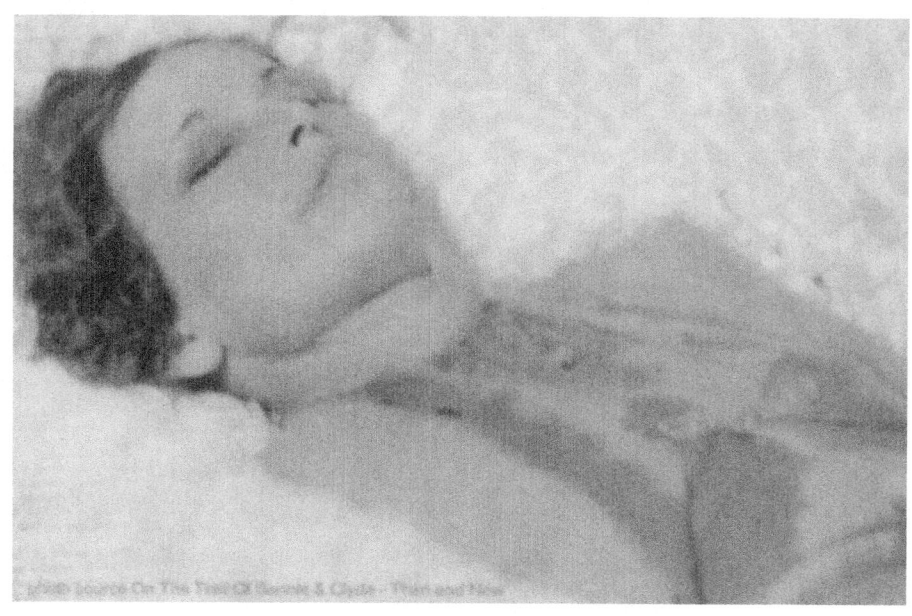

Thousands had lined the street at Forest Avenue to view the tiny shattered remains of Bonnie Parker

THE GRIEVING MOTHER

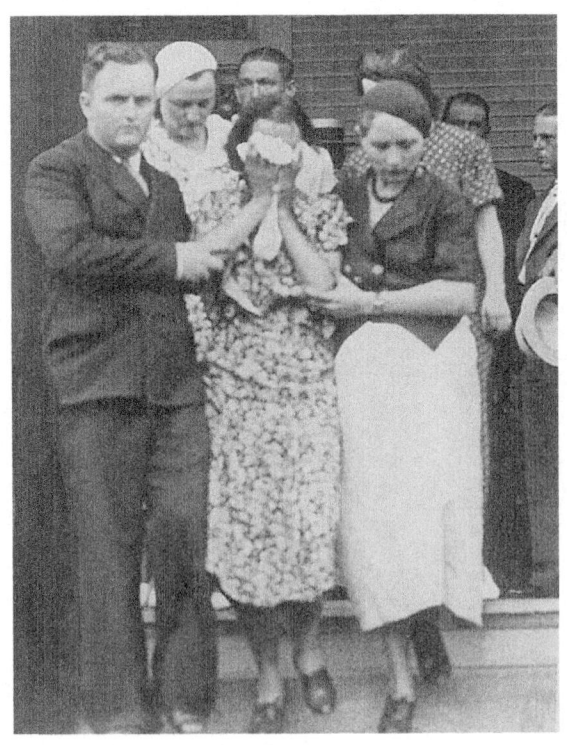

Hubert Parker supporting his mother, Emma

BARROW FUNERAL

Deaths and Funeral Notices

BARROW—Clyde, passed away at Gibsland, La., early Wednesday; survived by parents, Mr. and Mrs. Henry Barrow; two brothers, two sisters. Funeral arrangements to be announced later by Sparkman-Holtz-Brand.

SPARKMAN-HOLTZ-BRAND FUNERAL HOME

Photo above shows services held for Clyde Barrow in 1934.
Clyde's remains were carried to the Sparkman-Holtz-Brand Funeral Home
on Ross Avenue in Dallas attracting 30,000 visitors

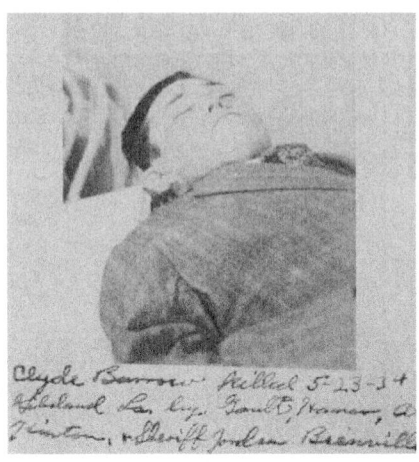

CLYDE BARROW LIES ON SLAB IN CONGER'S BACK ROOM

THE GRIEVING MOTHER

A frail Cummie Barrow being assisted

Bonnie Parker's grave, inscribed with: *As the flowers are all made sweeter by the sunshine and the dew, so this old world is made brighter by the lives of folks like you*

Bonnie and Clyde wished to be buried side by side, but the Parker family would not allow it. Mrs. Parker had wanted to grant her daughter's final wish, which was to be brought home, but the mobs surrounding the Parker house made that impossible. More than twenty thousand attended Bonnie Parker's funeral, making it difficult for her family to reach the grave site.

Parker's family used the now defunct McKamy-Campbell Funeral Home, then located on Forest Avenue (now Martin Luther King, Jr. Boulevard) in Dallas, to conduct her funeral. Hubert "Buster" Parker accompanied his sister's body back to Dallas in the McKamy-Campbell ambulance. Her services were held on Saturday, May 26, 1934, at 2 pm, in the funeral home, directed by Allen D. Campbell. His son, Dr. Allen Campbell, later remembered that flowers came from everywhere, including some with cards allegedly from Pretty Boy Floyd and John Dillinger. The largest floral tribute was sent by a group of Dallas city newsboys; the sudden end of Bonnie and Clyde sold 500,000 newspapers in Dallas alone. Soloists at the funeral included Dudley M Hughes, Sr., later the operator of four large funeral homes in Dallas. Although initially buried in the Fishtrap Cemetery, Parker was moved, in 1945, to the new Crown Hill Cemetery in Dallas. Services for Raymond Hamilton, a member of the Barrow Gang who was executed by the State of Texas on May 10, 1935, were also held at the McKamy-Campbell Funeral Home.

Barrow's family used the Sparkman-Holtz-Brand Morticians, located in the A.H. Belo mansion in downtown Dallas. Thousands of people gathered outside both Dallas funeral homes hoping for a chance to view the bodies. Barrow's private funeral was held at sunset on Friday, May 25, in the funeral home chapel. He was buried in Western Heights Cemetery in Dallas, next to his brother, Marvin. The Barrow brothers share a single granite marker with their names on it and a four-word epitaph previously selected by Clyde: "Gone but not forgotten." In 2013, Bob Phillips in his syndicated television series *Texas Country Reporter* visited the graves of both Bonnie and Clyde with the theme, "Crime does not pay".

The life insurance policies for both Bonnie Parker and Clyde Barrow were paid in full by American National of Galveston. Since then, the policy of pay-outs has changed to exclude pay-outs in cases of deaths caused by any criminal act by the insured.

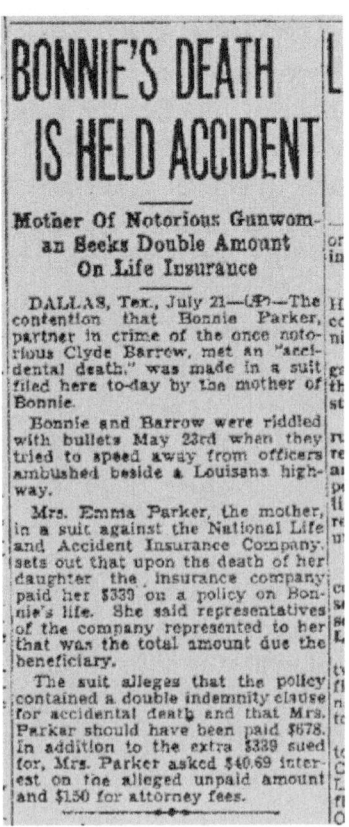

In addition to the memorabilia collected by the posse, the six men were each to receive a one-sixth share of the reward money. Dallas Sheriff Schmid had promised Ted Hinton this would total some $26,000, but most of the state, county, and other organizations that had pledged reward funds reneged on their pledges; by the time the six checks were issued to the possemen, each had earned just $200.23 for his efforts.

Clyde and Buck Barrow's grave, inscribed with: *Gone but not forgotten*

The ambush of Barrow and Parker proved to be the beginning of the end of the "public enemy era" of the 1930s. New federal statutes that made bank robbery and kidnapping federal offenses, the growing coordination of local jurisdictions by the FBI, and the installation of two-way radios in police cars combined to make the free-ranging outlaw bandit lifestyle much more difficult in the summer of 1934 than it had been just a few months before. Two months after Gibsland, John Dillinger was ambushed and killed on the street in Chicago; three months after that, Charles Arthur "Pretty Boy Floyd" took 14 FBI bullets in the back in Ohio; and one month after that, Lester "Baby Face Nelson" Gillis shot it out, and lost, in Illinois.

Controversies

Questions following the ambush were helped along by the tripartite composition of the posse itself: Hamer and Gault were both former Texas Rangers now working for the Texas Department of Corrections, Hinton and Alcorn were employees of the Dallas Sheriff's office, and Jordan and Oakley were Sheriff and Deputy of Bienville Parish. The three duos distrusted each other, kept to themselves, and indeed did not even much like each other. They each carried differing agendas into the operation and brought differing narratives out of it. Historian Guinn puts it this way:

"Hamer's, Simmons's, Jordan's and Hinton's various testimonies combine into one of the most dazzling displays of deliberate obfuscation in modern history. Such widely varied accounts can't be dismissed as different people honestly recalling the same events different ways. Motive becomes an issue, and they all had reason to lie. Hamer was fanatical about protecting sources. Simmons was interested in resurrecting his own public image ... Jordan wanted to present himself as the critical dealmaker. Nobody can account for Ted Hinton's improbable reminiscences ..."

Because their self-serving accounts vary so widely, and because all six men are long deceased, the exact details of the ambush are unknown and unknowable.

As a result, the questions have lingered, including whether fair warning was given the fugitives before the firing commenced, the status of Parker as a shoot-on-sight candidate, and the 1970s-era accusations of Deputy Hinton.

Over a dozen guns and several thousand rounds of ammunition (including 100 20-rounds BAR magazines) were in the perforated Ford.

Calling a "Halt!"

The efficacy of calling out a warning to Clyde Barrow before an ambush was demonstrated by Dallas Sheriff Schmid at Sowers, Texas in November 1933. At his call of "Halt!" there was a smattering of gunfire from the outlaw car, a sweeping U-turn, and then rapidly vanishing taillights: The ambush was over. Hinton later called it "the most futile gesture of the week. "When the two Louisiana officers on the posse assumed that calling "Halt!" would be the prelude to the bullets, the four Texans "vetoed the idea," hurrying to inform them that Clyde's history had always been to shoot his way out of seemingly hopeless entrapments, like Platte City, Dexfield Park, and Sowers. It is unlikely that Hamer planned to give any warning, but the matter became moot when Deputy Oakley simply stood up and opened fire; after a beat, the startled possemen joined him in the fusillade. In their descriptions of the event, Jordan said *he* called out to Barrow, Alcorn said Hamer called out, and Hinton claimed Alcorn did, while in another paper that same day, they *each* said they *both* did. These conflicting claims most likely were collegial attempts to divert the focus from their gun-jumping associate Oakley, who admitted in subsequent years that he fired prematurely.

Hinton's accusations

In 1979, Ted Hinton's as-told-to account of the ambush was published posthumously as *Ambush*, and it attempted to change the complexion of the Methvin family's involvement in the planning and execution of the ambush. According to Hinton, the posse had tied Henry Methvin's father, Ivy, to a tree the previous night, to keep him from possibly warning the outlaws off. Hamer, Hinton claimed, made Ivy Methvin a deal: keep quiet about being tied up, and his son would be pardoned for the murder of the two young highway patrolmen at Grapevine, a pardon which Henry Methvin did eventually receive. Hinton alleged that Hamer made every member of the posse swear they would never divulge this secret. Other accounts, however, place Methvin Senior at the very center of the action that morning, not tied up but right down on the road, waving for Clyde Barrow to stop—having cut Henry's pardon deal several weeks before. John Treherne posits a less sinister explanation: Hamer, he says, may well have floated the tied-to-a-tree scenario to give Ivy Methvin an "alibi" in the event that Barrow escaped the ambush or the family later wanted revenge against a betrayer. Hinton's odd memoir also propounds the tale that the offending stogie in the famous "cigar photo" of Bonnie had in fact been a *rose* in her mouth that was retouched *into* a cigar by darkroom personnel at the *Joplin Globe* while they were preparing the photo for publication. Guinn says that "some people who knew Hinton suspect he became delusional late in life."

Aftermath

The smoke from the fusillade had not even cleared before the posse began sifting through the items in the Barrow death car. Hamer appropriated the "considerable" arsenal of stolen guns and ammunition, plus a box of fishing tackle, under the terms of his compensation package with the Texas DOC. In July, Clyde's mother Cummie wrote to Hamer asking for the return of the guns: "You don't never want to forget my boy was never tried in no court for murder, and no one is guilty until proven guilty by some court so I hope you will answer this letter and also return the guns I am asking for." No record exists of any response.

Alcorn claimed Barrow's saxophone from the car, but feeling guilty, later returned it to the Barrow family. Other personal items such as Parker's clothing were also taken, and when the Parker family asked for them back, they were refused. These items were later sold as souvenirs. A rumored suitcase full of cash was said by the Barrow family to have been kept by Sheriff Jordan, "who soon after the ambush purchased an auction barn and land in Arcadia." Jordan also attempted to keep the death car for his own but found himself the target of a lawsuit by Ruth Warren of Topeka, the owner of the car from whom Barrow had stolen the vehicle on April 29; after considerable legal sparring and a court order, Jordan relented and the car was returned to Mrs. Warren in August 1934. It was still covered with blood and tissue. She had to pay an $85 towing and storage bill.

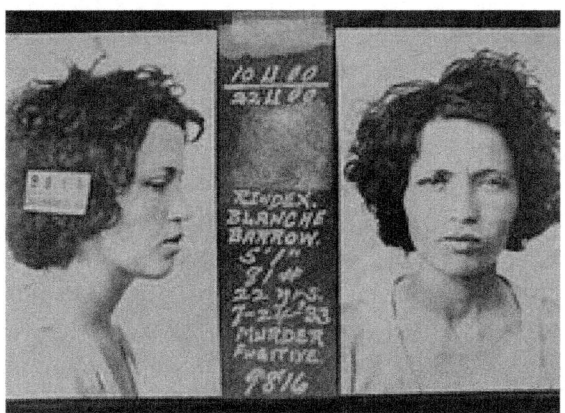

Blanche Barrow

Blanche spent the rest of the 1930s in prison for her four-month run with the gang; she weighed just 81 pounds when captured

In February 1935, Dallas and federal authorities conducted a "harboring trial" in which 20 family members and friends of the outlaw couple were arrested and jailed for the aid and abetment of Barrow and Parker. All twenty either pleaded or were found guilty. The two mothers were jailed for 30 days; other sentences ranged from two years' imprisonment for Raymond Hamilton's brother Floyd to one hour in custody for teenager Marie Barrow, Clyde's sister Other defendants included Blanche Barrow, W. D. Jones, Henry Methvin and Bonnie's sister Billie.

Blanche Barrow's injuries left her permanently blinded in her left eye. After the 1933 shootout at Dexfield Park, she was taken into custody on the charge of "Assault With Intent to Kill." She was sentenced to ten years in prison but was paroled in 1939 for good behavior. She returned to Dallas, leaving her life of crime in the past, and lived with her invalid father as his caregiver. She married Eddie Frasure in 1940, worked as a taxi cab dispatcher and a beautician, and completed the terms of her parole one year later. She lived in peace with her husband until he died of cancer in 1969. Warren Beatty approached her to purchase the rights to her name for use in the 1967 film *Bonnie and Clyde*. While she agreed to the original script, she objected to her characterization in the final film, describing Estelle Parsons's Academy Award-winning portrayal of her as "a screaming horse's ass." Despite this, she maintained a firm friendship with Beatty. She died from cancer at the age of 77 on December 24, 1988, and was buried in Dallas's Grove Hill Memorial Park under the name "Blanche B. Frasure".

Trouble and substance problems dogged W.D. Jones until his own murder in 1974

Barrow cohorts Raymond Hamilton and Joe Palmer, both Eastham escapees in January 1934, both recaptured, and both subsequently convicted of murder, shared one more thing in common: they were both executed in the electric chair, "Old Sparky", at Huntsville, Texas, and both on the same day: May 10, 1935.

Barrow protégé W. D. Jones had split from his mentors six weeks after the three slipped the noose at Dexfield Park in July 1933. He found his way to Houston and got a job picking cotton, where he was soon discovered and captured. He was returned to Dallas, where he dictated a "confession" in which he claimed to have been kept a prisoner by Barrow and Parker. Some of the more lurid embellishments he made concerned the gang's sex lives, and it was this testimony that gave rise to many of the stories about Barrow's ambiguous sexuality. Jones was convicted of the murder of Doyle Johnson and served a lenient sentence of fifteen years. He struggled for years with substance abuse problems, gave an interview to *Playboy* during the heyday of excitement surrounding the 1967 movie, and was killed on August 4, 1974 in a misunderstanding by the jealous boyfriend of a woman he was trying to help out.

Substitute protégé Henry Methvin's ambush-earned Texas pardon didn't help him in Oklahoma, where he was convicted of the 1934 murder of Constable Campbell at Commerce. He was paroled in 1942 and killed by a train in 1948; it was said he fell asleep, drunk, on the tracks, but there were rumors he had been pushed by parties seeking revenge for his betrayal of Clyde Barrow. His father Ivy had been killed in 1946 by a hit-and-run driver, and here too there was talk of foul play. Bonnie Parker's husband Roy Thornton was sentenced to five years in prison for burglary in March 1933. He was killed by guards on October 3, 1937, during an escape attempt from Eastham Farm prison.

In the years after the ambush, Prentiss Oakley, who all six possemen agree fired the first shots, was reported to have been troubled by his actions. He often admitted to his friends that he had fired prematurely and he was the only posse member to express regret publicly. He would go on to succeed Henderson Jordan as sheriff of Bienville Parish in 1940.

By 1967's Summer of Love, Penn's film gave the outlaws a new image for a new generation who had no personal recollection of the historical couple's bloody exploits some 33 years earlier

Frank Hamer returned to a quieter life as a freelance security consultant—a strikebreaker—to oil companies, although, according to Guinn, "his reputation suffered somewhat after Gibsland" because many people felt he had not given Barrow and Parker a fair chance to surrender. He made headlines again in 1948 when he and Governor Coke Stevenson unsuccessfully challenged Lyndon Johnson's vote totals during the election for the U.S. Senate. He died in 1955 at age 71 after several years of poor health. His posse mate Bob Alcorn died on May 23, 1964—exactly thirty years to the day after the Gibsland ambush.

On April 1, 2011, the 77th anniversary of the Grapevine murders, Texas Rangers, troopers and DPS staff presented the Yellow Rose of Texas commendation to Ella Wheeler-McLeod, 95, the last surviving sibling of highway patrolman Edward Bryan Wheeler, killed that Easter Sunday by the Barrow Gang. They presented McLeod, of San Antonio, with a plaque and framed portrait of her brother.

Ella Wheeler-McLeod, sister of highway patrolman Edward Bryan Wheeler, accepts the Yellow Rose of Texas award.

In the contemporary media

Bonnie Parker and Clyde Barrow were among the first celebrity criminals of the modern era. They had little choice in the matter: after they fled the Joplin hideout in April 1933 with nothing but the clothes they were wearing, the police discovered several rolls of undeveloped film and some scrawled doggerel poetry left behind. It was instant legend: the photos showed the couple and W. D. Jones in playful, snapshot-type poses, except they were wielding pistols, rifles and BARs. In one gag shot, Parker had plucked a cigar from Barrow and popped it in her mouth, branding her as "Clyde's cigar-smoking moll." The poem "Suicide Sal," peppered with quotation marks and colorful underworld vernacular, mirrored the tone of the popular detective magazines of the time. Two days after the raid, the photos and poem went out on the wire and were running in newspapers all over the country. Before Joplin, the Barrows' notoriety had been confined strictly to the Dallas area; afterwards, they became notorious across America.

The high public profile was a mixed blessing. It certainly made life on the run more dangerous and therefore more difficult. There were more nights sleeping in the car and fewer sleeping in motor courts; picking up laundry at cleaning stores was particularly harrowing. As the noose tightened, Parker composed the fatalistic poem she titled "The Trail's End," known since as "The Story of Bonnie and Clyde." She gave the handwritten ode to her mother upon their final meeting two weeks before her death and Emma Parker gave it to the press thereafter.

Six weeks before the couple was ambushed, a letter purportedly written by Barrow arrived at the office of

Henry Ford praising his "dandy car." Although the handwriting does not match known samples of Clyde's penmanship, and despite the fact the letter was signed by "Clyde *Champion* Barrow" while Barrow's middle name was *Chestnut*, the unauthenticated letter is on display in the Ford Museum

> Tulsa Okla
> 10th April
>
> Mr. Henry Ford
> Detroit Mich.
>
> [RECEIVED APR 13 1934]
>
> Dear Sir:—
>
> While I still have got breath in my lungs I will tell you what a dandy car you make. I have drove Fords exclusively when I could get away with one. For sustained speed and freedom from trouble the Ford has got every other car skinned, and even if my business hasn't been strictly legal it don't hurt eny thing to tell you what a fine car you got in the V8 —
>
> Yours truly
> Clyde Champion Barrow

It was never used in any form in Ford advertising, nor was a similar letter Ford received around the same time that was presumed to have come from Dillinger, himself ambushed just two months after Barrow.

The Bonnie and Clyde Festival

Every year near the anniversary of the ambush, a "Bonnie and Clyde Festival" is hosted in the town of Gibsland, off Interstate 20 in Bienville Parish. The ambush location, still comparatively isolated on Louisiana Highway 154, south of Gibsland, is commemorated by a stone marker that has been defaced to near illegibility by souvenir hunters and gunshot. A small metal version was added to accompany the stone monument. It was stolen, as was its replacement.

Souvenir hunters have ravaged several memorial stones at the rural ambush site.

In Closing…

Well here we are at the end of the Ride. There are still so many things that could be said and so many crimes that the authorities believe Bonnie and Clyde committed but where never charged for. I could sit here and try to figure this all out but instead I will end this with a section dedicated to the victims and their families. May God bless each and every one of them.

This section is dedicated to the memory of the twelve victims of
Bonnie and Clyde

John N. Bucher of Hillsboro, Texas: Died April 30, 1932

Eugene Moore of Atoka, Oklahoma: Died August 5, 1932

Howard Hall of Sherman, Texas: Died October 11, 1932

Doyle Johnson of Temple, Texas: Died December 26, 1932

Malcolm Davis of Dallas, Texas: Died January 6, 1933

Harry McGinnis of Joplin, Missouri: Died April 13, 1933

Wes Harriman of Joplin, Missouri: Died April 13, 1933

Henry D. Humphrey of Alma, Arkansas: Died June 26, 1933

Major Crowson of Huntsville, Texas: Died January 16, 1934

E.B. Wheeler of Grapevine, Texas: Died April 1, 1934

H.D. Murphy of Grapevine, Texas: Died April 1, 1934

Cal Campbell of Commerce, Oklahoma: Died April 6, 1934

Look for these and other great books By David Pietras

From "Mommy to Monster"

The "Daddy Dearest" Club

The Manson Family "Then and Now"

When Love Kills

The Making of a Nightmare

THE INFAMOUS "FLORIDA 5"

Death, Murder, and Vampires Real Vampire Stories

The Life and Death of Richard Ramirez, The Night Stalker (History's Killers Unmasked Series)

Profiling The Killer of a Childhood Beauty Queen

No Justice For Caylee Anthony

A Texas Style Witch Hunt "Justice Denied" The Darlie Lynn Routier Story by

The Book of Revelations Explained The End Times

Murder of a Childhood

John Gotti: A True Mafia Don (History's Killers Unmasked Series)

MURDERED FOR HIS MILLIONS The Abraham Shakespeare Case

The Son of Sam "Then and Now" The David Berkowitz Story

A LOOK INSIDE THE FIVE MAFIA FAMILIES OF NEW YORK CITY

Unmasking The Real Hannibal Lecter

Top 10 Most Haunted Places in America

40 minutes in Abbottabad The Raid on Osama bin Laden

In The Footsteps of a Hero The Military Journey of General David H. Petraeus

BATTLEFIELD BENGHAZI

CASE CLOSED The State of Florida vs. George Zimmerman THE TRUTH REVEALED

CROSSING THE THIN BLUE LINE

THE GHOST FROM MY CHILDHOOD A TRUE GHOST STORY ABOUT THE GELSTON CASTLE AND THE GHOST OF "AUNT" HARRIET DOUGLAS...

Haunted United Kingdom

In Search of Jack the Ripper (History's Killers Unmasked Series)

The Last Ride of Bonnie and Clyde

The Meaning of a Tragedy Canada's Serial Killers Revealed

MOMSTER

Murder In The Kingdom

The Shroud of Turin and the Mystery Surrounding Its Authenticity

The Unexplained World That We Live In

Printed in Dunstable, United Kingdom